Broken
BEAUTY

reflections of a soul refined by cancer

"The kingdom of heaven is like a merchant looking for fine pearls. When he found one of great value, he went away and sold everything he had and bought it."

MATTHEW 13:45–46

BROKEN BEAUTY
Reflections of a Soul Refined by Cancer

Wipf & Stock
An Imprint of Wipf and Stock Publishers
199 W. 8th Ave., Suite 3
Eugene, OR 97401

www.wipfandstock.com

PAPERBACK ISBN: 978-1-7252-6659-9
HARDCOVER ISBN: 978-1-7252-6660-5
EBOOK ISBN: 978-1-7252-6661-2

This title is also available in an audio edition.

Manufactured in the U.S.A.

for You, Father,

for Your glory

Contents

The Comforter

Oh! Thou who dry'st the mourner's tear,
How dark this world would be,
If, when deceived and wounded here,
We could not fly to Thee!

The friends who in our sunshine live,
When winter comes are flown;
And he who has but tears to give,
Must weep those tears alone;

But Thou wilt heal that broken heart,
Which, like the plants that throw
Their fragrance from the wounded part,
Breathes sweetness out of woe.

When joy no longer soothes or cheers,
And even the hope that threw
A moment's sparkle o'er our tears,
Is dimm'd and vanish'd too;

Oh who would bear life's stormy doom,
Did not Thy wing of love
Come brightly wafting through the gloom,
Our peace-branch from above.

Then sorrow, touch'd by Thee, grows bright
With more than rapture's ray;
As darkness shows us worlds of light
We never saw by day.

Thomas Moore

Preface

For our light and momentary troubles are achieving for us an eternal glory that far outweighs them all.

2 CORINTHIANS 4:17

Before you begin to read this book, I wish to clarify my intentions. The objective of my writing is not to place cancer on the highest pedestal of suffering, as if it represents the epitome of all affliction. Everyone suffers in one way or another as we live our lives East of Eden. We're in a world that's broken, after all.

And so, although I certainly had cancer patients and their families in mind while writing this book, I pray it may also bring some comfort and encouragement to those suffering other ailments or situations, whether they be of a mental, physical, or spiritual nature.

No two journeys are alike. No two people are alike. Reactions and needs will always vary, but I hope that the pages of *Broken Beauty* will help those of you who are suffering and those of you who are providing love and support to them.

To the diagnosed pilgrims: I pray that this book helps you to be strong and of good courage and that, through your brokenness, the beauty of the glory of God may shine.

To those who have never stopped to ponder what refining is all about: Do use this book as a reminder to prepare yourself for the day you will be refined. And make no mistake. You, too, will in God's perfect time and in God's perfect way walk through the fire. It happens to all those whom the Father loves.

A final consideration before you begin reading: all cancer patients suffer, some much more than others. My journey was relatively easy compared to many. I know. I've met them. Spoken to them. Held their hands. Prayed for them. So, let's not waste time or energy weighing suffering on a scale to see whose is the greatest. Rather, let's use the scale to measure the weight of glory on the other side. Our troubles are then weighed in the right balance.

With love in Christ,

Helena Bolhuis
Perth, Western Australia, 2020

PART ONE:

THE JOURNEY

For from Him and through Him and for Him are all things.
To Him be the glory forever!

ROMANS 11:36

Let me tell you my story. But it's not really my story. It's God's story in my story. It's His glory in my story. And so, my story was written as a context for His. He is, after all, where things come from, where things go through, and Whom things are ultimately for. He's where things begin, where things are, and where things will be. God is where everything comes together perfectly.

May His story in mine encourage and equip you, dear reader, to travel the days of your journey in His strength and with hope in His purposes, knowing that your story, too, forms part of His greater story. With God's gracious provisions, we can all fulfill the aim of our very existence: "To glorify God, and to enjoy Him for ever."[1]

As you begin to read, my heartfelt prayer is that *Broken Beauty* will meet you where you are at, and that you will uncover on its pages the treasure of God's glory to be found in your story. As a result of this uncovering, may you experience intimacy with God that leads you to joy, which transcends your circumstance.

---

[1] *Westminster Shorter Catechism*, Question and Answer 1.

One

The Diagnosis

Be still.

PSALM 46:10

I didn't get it, even though the words were right in front of me.

The card I received shortly after my breast cancer diagnosis simply read:

May God receive the glory.

I struggled for comprehension, but came up empty. Didn't this friend realize that my entire world had just collapsed? What was she writing about glory for! I was in survival mode and all she could think about was God's glory?

But we're getting ahead of ourselves. Let's go back to a month before I received the "glory" card. It's summer holidays, and my husband and I, along with our six children, are at our favorite place: camping opposite the most beautiful beach God had ever breathed into existence. No one has a care in the world when you're in the waves—anxieties leave, pressures ease, and it's just you and those you love basking in the creation of the Creator.

Well, okay, maybe there's a slight worry. Even though I tried, I couldn't quite get out of my mind the biopsy that was performed a few weeks earlier. They said it was just a precaution due to the mammogram having picked up dots that hadn't been on my previous image. But would they ask me to come in to discuss the findings if it was just a precaution? Maybe it was just as well that I had asked my pastor's wife to pray for me. Because maybe those dots were something else! Then again, maybe I was escalating a situation that didn't even exist. I felt like I was on a precipice, not knowing what lay a few steps ahead.

The morning of the appointment for my biopsy results dawned like any other day. After breakfast, my husband picked up our kids' devotion book and opened it randomly to the wrong date (we were on holidays after all!). And there it was: Psalm 46—a psalm that spoke about being still, even if the mountains were plunging into the sea. The corresponding devotion communicated how God's Word was to be the immovable foundation of our lives, no matter what may happen to us—that His Word was kind of like tent pegs that kept your tent from blowing away in a storm.

I started to feel slightly uncomfortable. Little things were beginning to form a bigger picture: the mammogram, the biopsy, and now this Psalm being read right before it was time to leave for my appointment. I tried to push my unease aside and see this trip as a special outing of a mother with her oldest son. My husband and I had decided that since he needed some driving experience in order to obtain his license, my son could take me to and from the appointment, an hour's journey each way. My husband would use the opportunity to enjoy a day with our other five children at a nearby attraction. I told him not to rush back, even though I was sure I wouldn't be long. I could just read my book at the campsite while waiting for them to return. Surely the test results would show nothing and I could handle this appointment on my own, my confident self insisted. This would all be over before it started and life would carry on as normal.

So, off my firstborn and I went. It was a hot day, as most summer days in Western Australia are, and I enjoyed the drive in. When we got to the clinic my son found himself a book to read in the waiting room while I was shown into the office. As I entered and looked at the faces of the nurse and the doctor, my heart started to pound and my vision started to blur. Events began unfolding in slow-motion. Before I could stop them, I heard the three words that would forever change my life: "You have cancer."

It felt like a physical blow! Like I had been hit by a truck, kicked in the stomach, knocked over the head all at the same time. I felt myself detaching from my body. What did the doctor just say? I tried to catch up to the world spinning around me, because now, instead of events progressing in slow-motion, things were moving incredibly fast: diagrams were being brought out and the doctor was speaking and it was probably all really important so I had to pay attention. Mustering all my mental strength, I forced my mind back to the present and started hearing words like "caught early," "very small area," "just a quick operation and you'll be fine." With these words ringing in my ears I was told an appointment for an hour's time had already been made to see a breast cancer surgeon.

Before I could stop them, I heard the three words that would forever change my life: "You have cancer."

When I returned to the waiting room and saw my son's face crumple when he saw mine, my world began to tilt once again. Maybe coffee in the cafeteria with him would be a good idea. We sat at one of their outside tables, no longer noticing what a beautiful day it was. I spoke the words that had been unsaid but understood moments before in the waiting room. I had cancer. I saw him trying to comprehend the enormity of the incomprehensible. Saw him reaching for words that struggled to pass his lips: "But Jane McGrath died of breast cancer."[2]

And so, there we sat, in the hospital cafeteria, with the January sunshine all around us, my son, and me. Hazes of memory drifted through my mind—the original mammogram and biopsy, confiding to my pastor's wife, praying with my husband and putting this appointment in God's hands while at the same time telling myself it was nothing, and just this morning, the reading of Psalm 46. In retrospect, the signs were all there, perhaps even the possibility of this diagnosis existed in my mind, but my heart never let it gain traction. Wasn't cancer something you read about in the church bulletin as happening to someone else? You prayed for that someone else, maybe sent a card, or dropped off a meal. But cancer wasn't something that happened to you. Or was it?

An hour later it was time for the appointment with the breast surgeon. How ludicrous this all seemed! My body and mind felt like they were at odds with one another as my son and I entered yet another waiting room. But then I began to get the first, tiniest, slightest glimmer of what this journey was to be all about.

The pinprick of light began with the compassion I saw on the face of the surgeon's receptionist. This was no nine to fiver, "just tell me when it's Friday" type of receptionist. Even in my haze, I recognized that fact immediately. She must have seen the turmoil on my face as she reached out to reassure me, telling me while pointing to the surgeon's office, that I had a fantastic physician assigned to me. The tilt in my brain lessened somewhat and a moment of clarity of sorts entered my thinking. I, too, pointed, not to the doctor's door, but rather to the heavens and answered: "God is my Great Physician." "Yes," the receptionist replied, "but he works for Him." The pinprick of light began to intensify.

---

[2] Jane McGrath died of breast cancer in 2008. She was the wife of Australian cricket fast bowler, Glenn McGrath.

As I entered the office of the doctor, things still felt surreal. My confusion multiplied as the original cancer diagnosis was modified then and there into a pre-cancer diagnosis. What on earth was that anyways? I began to feel like I needed a university degree to get a handle on what exactly was even happening. My brain was in such a fog it took every last effort of my self-discipline to focus on what the doctor was trying to say.

And so, as he began talking about booking in for surgery the following week, the importance of clear margins, possibilities of lymph node involvement, the high grade of my pre-cancer and the important information the postsurgical pathology results would provide, I felt like I was drowning. I frantically reminded myself to breathe. You mean I've got bad cells multiplying in my body right at this minute? Operations, test results, radiation were all words that assaulted while I worked desperately to pull myself together.

Where had my normal world gone? It was there a few hours ago! I feverishly searched my purse for a pen so I could make some notes because I knew that when I left this room I would remember nothing besides this sick feeling in my stomach. I willed myself to write something down so I would know how to explain this to my family back at the campsite.

The campsite.

That seemed so long ago, so far away. My husband and children didn't even know that everything had changed! My realities were not lining up. I felt disoriented.

But then I started to calm. My out-of-control feelings didn't mean things were out of control. And so, through the blur of words the doctor delivered—words he had delivered so many times to so many other patients before, but never to me—a semblance of peace dawned and, astonishingly, Bible texts began to form in the subconsciousness of my mind's intellect. Where were they coming from? Perhaps from this morning's Bible reading where God told me that He would be my refuge. Perhaps from the devotion series

I'd read a few months ago about the importance of preparation for refining. Perhaps from the whispering of God's Spirit in my heart, reminding me of biblical truths—truths taught from childhood, truths that I believed, but now truths that I would live.

I was still swimming in the crashing waves, flailing about and not really understanding how I got here or how this happened, but I was beginning to comprehend that God was near, and that He would be beside me through the storm. This comprehension would prove to be a process, a dawning realization, something that would ebb and flow, but yes, praise God, it would be there consistently—God's presence in the midst of the tempest.

There was absolutely no way I would be able to walk this journey alone, but that was all right, because as the Light expanded from its pinprick, I realized I wasn't alone anyways. Despite the bewildering words whirling around me, its rays were there in the eye of the storm. I wasn't sure what the Light had planned, but Light in the darkness it was and I grasped at it and hung on to it for dear life. And for the first time I thought maybe, just maybe, this was all going to be okay.

So, with tears in my eyes but a gradual emergence of peace in my heart, I left the surgeon's office, my world changed, while everyone else's seemed to continue as normal.

After completing preadmission paperwork for my operation scheduled for the following week, my son and I began our journey back to the campsite to tell my husband and children that the course of their lives was about to change radically. To convey to them that the genesis of my journey was the genesis of theirs and that I was unsure where God was taking us or for how long the journey would last. As we began to drive, I realized, with increasing certainty as the kilometers faded behind us, that God was leading this expedition, and I was following.

Cancer. This was the beginning of the battle. A battle not to be fought just in my body, but also in my soul. It would prove over the course of time to be a battle that would require confrontation on many fronts—relational, mental, emotional, physical, and spiritual—taking me and others along with me to the very limit of our endurance. Already now I could see that the threads on God's weaving loom were not to be woven on my tapestry alone. My cancer would not leave anyone in my sphere untouched.

But the part of the journey that would prove of greatest import would be the spiritual metamorphosis I was about to undergo. Maybe it was good I realized so little of this at the time, or otherwise the implications of it all would have surely overwhelmed me.

My thoughts turned to my husband, sure to be back by now from his outing with the other children. How would I ever tell him my astonishing news? How would I tell my children? The shock and pain I was feeling was something I was about to unleash on the very people I loved the most. And I didn't want to do it. I didn't think I could do it. And try as I might to desperately regain my earlier perspective that just maybe things would be okay, my mind did battle with images of my own funeral, my husband and children sitting in the front church pew looking at my casket. I remembered then what my surgeon had answered when asked how best to break this news to my husband and children: "Just tell them. If they have faith in God like you do, it will be okay," he had said.

We arrived back at the campsite with the sun beginning to go down. Everything looked the same as when we left, yet everything was different. There was no going back. Results had been given. A surgeon had been assigned. An operation had been booked. My world had changed, and I was about to change the world of those I loved most. I took my husband's hand and led him to a bench overlooking the endless ocean, its horizon promising a beautiful sunset. I told him the news.

We watched the waves rolling in, one after another. There's a rhythm in the waves that resonates the unchanging nature of God so powerfully. True, the mountains may have fallen into the heart of the sea, our entire world was tilting off its axis, but God was there, our ever-present refuge and strength. It was time to be still. And know. He is God. And somehow, it would all have to be okay.

Hi Helena,

Bill heard from your brother that you have received some devastating news recently . . . a breast cancer diagnosis! I can tell you from my own experience that those first few weeks are extremely difficult, but once the shock wears off it does get easier. I was dx'd on August 8th and a month later had my surgery. John mentioned that you are having surgery soon? In my case, having the surgery was a big relief . . . I just wanted the tumor out and a plan of action to follow.

I hope and pray that your surgery goes well and that the cancer is contained. If you would like to ask me any questions you have maybe I can be of help since I have gone before you by a few months. I just had my sixth chemo treatment today, and two more to go, so I am seeing a small light at the end of the tunnel. I won't lie to you and say that it has been easy, but with God's help I take it one day at a time and try not to imagine the worst. As God has carried me this far He will carry you as well, and what a comfort that is, in fact He is our only comfort!

So dear cousin, one day at a time and don't think the worst, is my advice. God is faithful, and He will turn this to your good, as He has promised us in His Word! Feel free to ask me anything, I've learned a lot in these months and I know I had a lot of unanswered questions in the beginning.

Love, Caroline

Caroline,

Thank you so much for your message. When I read it I cried, which I hadn't really done up to that point. I praise God for many things on my journey so far, including the early diagnosis that could be made. It is very early breast cancer. It's called DCIS high grade, which means cancer in the milk duct. It is most likely contained, so a surgery Wednesday and if they get clean margins, six weeks of radiation. My surgeon is a Christian, another reason for thankfulness.

I have found the hardest thing so far is telling others. It is very emotionally draining. So although our church community is a very small and close one, I am leaving it to our pastor to tell the news to them on Sunday. I have just let family and very close friends know for now. I find it hard to answer really personal questions about it (some people can be blunt when asking about what the surgeon is going to do . . .). I, too, am looking forward to the surgery being over and done with. I'm not good with hospitals, etc, and the biopsy was not a nice introduction to it all!!

We continue to hold you in our prayers and thank you for doing the same. We pray God gives you strength to finish the chemo treatments and that all those terrible cancer cells will be gone out of your body forever. We're clinging to God's promises of turning all things to our good and we know He has a plan with this too. His ways are not always our ways, and although I prayed I and my family wouldn't have to go through this, in this instance God's answer was No, and we accept that. It is all a little overwhelming right now, so I'm trying to take things day by day and trying hard not to worry too much about tomorrow.

Love, Helena

Two

The Waiting Game

I will lift up my eyes to the hills.

P S A L M 1 2 1 : 1 (NKJV)

The words echoed off the walls of the surgeon's office a week after the operation. The pathology results had come back and the news wasn't good. The doctor would have to operate again and take more pre-cancerous cells away. *More.* More bad news, more sharing bad news, more operations, more waiting for results in waiting rooms. I felt like I was on a roller-coaster ride, not knowing whether I was up or down, not knowing how long the ride would be or even if I would make it through safely. Did I even have a say in any of this?

My mind retraced the events of the last few weeks.

It hadn't even been a month since D-day: Diagnosis Day. So much had happened since then, so much intensity. Telling the children after returning home from camping and seeing the confusion and fear on their faces was difficult. I was their Mom, their stability, their world. What was I doing changing all of that? I had tried to explain to them what cancer was, but truth be told, I didn't even understand it myself! And once the "c" word was said to the children, there was no going back. Their lives had completely changed in an instant. There are no words to describe how it feels as a mother having to destabilize the lives of your children.

The circle of those knowing continued to increase. Next came relaying the news to parents and siblings. One of the hardest moments was telling my elderly parents. How on earth do you do something like that from the other side of the world, anyways? I was in Australia, they lived in Canada. In the end, I asked my siblings to go to their house. I used Skype to impart the news across oceans and continents and waited for the moment of impact. Seeing them absorb the blow was difficult, but, again, there was light. As a family, with my father leading in prayer, we came before our Heavenly Father to ask for help. It had been a while since our family had prayed together. I felt a unity of faith with them in that moment, and was thankful for this silver lining.

And so, the ripples of the news had unrelentingly spread, engulfing others with shock, pain, and confusion. But there was more to go. On Sunday, on my forty-fifth birthday, the news was announced by our pastor to our small church community. As one body, we came before God's throne and prayed. Again, hearing the words out loud made things so much more real, almost as if not saying them could still make the whole thing go away.

Seeing the shock on peoples' faces after church had surprised me for some reason. I'm not sure why. Perhaps because we were such a close-knit community I subconsciously assumed that they would just know. After all, we had done everything together: our families had grown up together, we had shared years of Bible study together, we had carpooled everywhere together. But in reality, of course, they couldn't have known. Most likely my surprise had more to do with the fact that I had already started to process the events that had turned my world upside down. My church family were still at the impact stage. Had having cancer already begun to become normal to me in a strange sort of way?

As my news had radiated, upsetting many other lives, God had begun to show me in those weeks that the refining He was undertaking in my soul would produce heat that would also generate secondary refinements; that the reason God allowed cancer in my life had simultaneous purpose in others' lives as well and that together He wanted us to learn from what we were going through. To learn about surrender, about the power of prayer, about His sovereignty, about our responsibility. This was to be just the tip of the iceberg.

My mind returned to the present. It was time to prepare for my MRI[3] test and the operation that would follow. The test would determine the extent of the pre-cancer, in order to help the surgeon know what additional tissue to remove. A lot was at stake here. It was time to give the persistent praying widow a run for her money.[4] I was going to pray so hard that God would have to say "yes" to healing me, that this next test and operation would solve all my problems, get rid of all those nasty cells in my body and everyone could forget the last month had even happened. Life could go back to the "normal" I so craved and worshipped. So petition I did, all the while with my surgeon's words ringing in my ears: "You can't fight God, you know."

Ten days later saw me back at the hospital for my MRI results. It seemed my prayer plan was working! The MRI showed that the first operation had nearly gotten everything it needed to get! This meant that the second foray into the operating theatre would just be a cleanup mission. The light at the end of my well constructed tunnel was in sight. I could do this! If the pathology results after this operation showed that the area around the site (called the margins) was clear of any bad cells, it would simply mean a bit of radiation and then my life would be like everyone else's once again! And so, I was ready and in good spirits entering theatre for the second time a month after the first.

---

[3] Magnetic Resonance Imaging.

[4] The Parable of the Persistent Widow can be found in Luke 18:1–8.

My feeling of being back in control made it a little easier awaiting operation results this time around. I could almost anticipate my surgeon's words: "All clear—off you go to radiation." Ahh, wouldn't my children be relieved. All that pre-cancer tissue gone!

A week after my second surgery, my husband and I entered the doctor's office. My husband had begun coming with me to every appointment and test and it was so reassuring to have him by my side.

My doctor was about to leave for a month-long holiday the very next day, and so my husband happily walked into his office and said that he probably only had one thing on his mind: his holiday! The doctor didn't answer, just simply looked at us both. The kicked-in-the-stomach feeling that had only just started to dissipate after the MRI findings came back instantly and forcefully. The words didn't have to be said. My doctor's face gave it all away. Three of the four margins contaminated, and traces of invasive cancer were found among the pre-cancerous cells.

Through the haze I saw my doctor sliding a book across his desk to me, a book with an image of a woman on the cover that I was nowhere near ready to look at. I turned it over and slid it right back to him. There was no way that that woman was ever going to be me.

This was not good. This was not what we expected or prayed for.

This is what God gave us. This is what we had to work with.

The refining heat had been turned up a notch. And was I ever feeling it! I no longer felt confident. I no longer felt any semblance of control. The nurse took me to a private room and the floodgates opened and the tears flowed freely. I knew what this meant: there was no other way forward. I had to prepare myself for an operation that would alter me physically, for losing a part of my body that I couldn't begin to fathom losing.

Please, God, not me. Not my body.

We went home to our beautiful property in the country, and, as I stood by my kitchen window, lifting my eyes toward the hills, seeing the majestic Red Gum trees with the late afternoon sunshine gilding their brilliant canopies, I knew that cancer wasn't controlled by the doctor, wasn't controlled by test results, wasn't controlled by any rulebook, but was something controlled by God. He had heard my persistent prayers but had better plans for me: for my body but, more importantly, for my soul. And His plans were better than my plans, His ways better than my ways.

Things began to gradually, but steadily, change after this second shockwave. I became aware that this was not going to be a quick stroll in the park. God is not a random God, and this cancer was not something that He just decided to put in my life for a while and then return me to my prior condition afterwards. I was being changed, radically and powerfully. I started to wonder whether my life before this had been one big preparation: that all my years of relationship with God, of studying the Bible to find out Who He is and who I am, that all my understanding of biblical theology, was about to be tried and tested on the pages of my life like never before.

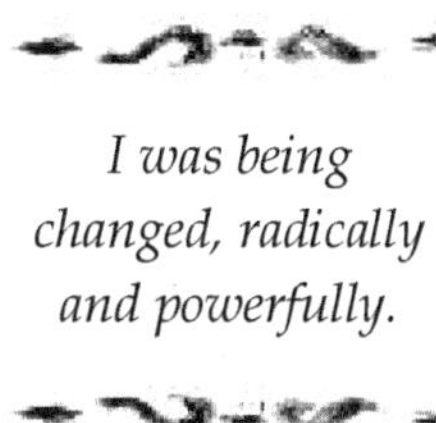

So, in His strength, I began to make changes—spiritual and physical ones. Both would be required to sustain me for what lay ahead.

Spiritual changes included room in my prayers for God's plan, and not simply my demands. Room for thanking Him for what He had already done, not just asking Him to do more. Room for asking for peace as I faced an unknown temporal existence while, at the same time, a known eternal one. These changes led me to spend much more meditative time in God's presence and, over time, meditation became critical to my very existence. It was no longer treated as an optional activity. Time in God's Word and Presence was water for my thirsty soul and, without it, I knew I would die spiritually in this desert march.

I began to see that I couldn't maintain a relationship with God while rushing from pillar to post, like everything else I did. Time with Him, digesting food from Him, was so much more than just a fast-food run. Just like my body had to be fed with nourishing food, so did my soul. Seeking God's face became my number one priority. I knew I couldn't go it alone.

It dawned on me that I needed to wait on the LORD, not just wait for test results. I needed to surrender to Him while I was in the dark about what my test results would bring to light. I couldn't live from test to test and be thrown about with no one to anchor me. I needed to live by faith, not by sight. Every time I waited for results, I needed to trust! Only this total trust could lead to total peace. Our wedding text often came to mind during this time of spiritual change: "Our soul waits for the LORD; He is our help and shield. Yea, our heart is glad in Him, because we trust in His holy name. Let Thy steadfast love, O LORD, be upon us, even as we hope in Thee" (Psalm 33:20–22 RSV).

I needed to hope in the LORD, knowing that He could do immeasurably more than all I asked or imagined (Ephesians 3:20–21). I needed God's Word and promises with me at all times. I could no longer go to appointments or tests without them. So, to help me remember, I began to print out Bible texts and tape them all over my cancer file (a file containing all my paperwork which I took to every appointment). Over time, more and more Bible texts appeared on this pink file, helping me remember God's promises so I could pray them as I waited for whatever the outcomes of the tests or visits would be.

As a result, I grew in hope. Not hope that I would be cured, although this was my prayer. But hope that believed God knew what He was doing regardless of how things unfolded. My hope was maturing into a hope that transcended my circumstances.

I also began making physical changes. I had always looked after my body, being quite active and eating well, but exercise and diet took on a whole new dimension as I realized that physically my body needed to be as strong as it could be to endure the onslaught of interventions that were on the horizon.

Yes, the results of the operation were in and there was no changing them. This was not going to be easy. But it was time. Time to not only walk in the story God had written for me and my family, but to embrace it as a means of spiritual growth. My pastor reminded me to walk forward one step at a time, through one door at a time, and not to be anxious about future doors I may need to walk through. God's mercies would be new again each morning (Lamentations 3:23). I needed to walk one day at a time in God's strength, going forward in faith, not fear, going forward not anticipating things, but trusting things were happening just the way they were meant to.

My covenant God was here, with me, changing me, all the while with His everlasting arms underneath me (Deuteronomy 33:27). It was time to find my will in God's will, to pray like Jesus did in the Garden, praying for the cup to pass, while knowing it might not pass at all. Learning to pray, like He taught: "Your will be done" (Matthew 26:42).

As I turned to my kitchen window once again and lifted my eyes, I saw the hills, with the afternoon sun changing them to fields of gold. I felt the light of the Son shining on me and I recalled the words of comfort and peace found in Psalm 121: "The LORD will keep you from all harm—He will watch over your life; the LORD will watch over your coming and going both now and forevermore" (v7–8).

And I knew. My foot would not slip. Not with my Helper by my side.

Dear Helena,

I was very saddened to read your news, not only because of the road that you must follow, but because it placed me right back to the time that I received my diagnosis. I have to say that this (breakdown of the diagnosis) was the hardest part of the whole journey, and when I was told that things would seem better once my treatment started, I didn't really believe it. However, this did come about, and now I am telling you the same thing that I was told. I believe that every day God supplies you with the strength for that day, and if you take one day at a time, and not look at the whole journey, it will seem a lot easier. I am by no means at the end of my journey against breast cancer, but when I look back I know that I am in a more secure place. I have received so much support from my faith, my family and my friends, and I am confident that you will receive the same.

Also, what I said in a previous email: don't assume the worst (which isn't so bad if you really think about it in a biblical way) will happen. I know I had to stop myself whenever I would dwell on this, however I do believe that some spiritual contemplation is needed, and this gets stronger as the time passes. I had a wonderful mentor that went through this journey a year ahead of me, and without her I would have had a much harder time dealing with everything. In fact, I believe that God used her disease for my good…and I pray that I might do the same for you. I will continue my prayers for you and your family. Take comfort in God's promises (our sermon this afternoon was on the text in Romans 8:28 "And we know that in all things God works for the good of those who love Him") and that includes diseases like cancer!

With love, your cousin, Caroline

Dear Caroline,

It was so nice to receive an email from you, as I really was in a place where I needed it. The compassion that came across warmed my heart. We're really trying not to let our highs be too high or our lows too low with this cancer journey, but to have the MRI so totally out and to not only hear that the margins are contaminated, but also about the invasion beginning was a little much to take in. Thankfully God gave us the peace in the appointment that we needed.

So we have given this over to the LORD, again, and feel His peace in our hearts. Again though, the hardest part for me is telling and supporting others. Telling my Mom & Dad and our children ranked super difficult. I know I need to entrust them to God's care, just like I've entrusted myself to His care. I think that is a process and God will have to carry me across that threshold.

I really felt comforted when you wrote that the breakdown of your diagnosis was the hardest part of the whole journey. I'm hoping that's true, because I am finding this rough going. All the testing, waiting, revising of plans. I just really want to get on with things now.

I know what you mean – and it's very good advice – not to worry about what may happen or to assume the worst. Well, the Bible also tells us not to worry about tomorrow and my doctor also reminds me of this, to take it a step at a time. I guess that's also true because things can change quickly. For example, I most likely will not have radiation now so worrying about that before would have done no good. However, I also think it's important to face your mortality, talk about it but then don't dwell on it. We have done this and it was in a way quite beautiful.

A blessing from this journey has been (amongst others) that our marriage has grown from a happy and good marriage to . . . I don't know how to say it—a marriage where we have become real soul mates. I thank God every day for the man standing beside me through this.

Really special that you were mentored the same way you are mentoring me. My pastor would call that "spreading the balm of God's Word over others' wounds." Speaking of pastors, thanks so much for posting that sermon link on Facebook about God turning things to good for those who love Him. What a fantastic sermon. I was so encouraged by it. I understand what the pastor means when he talks about a metamorphosis. I feel that happening to me. And it's a good thing, although I must say before I didn't think I needed metamorphosing!! I guess that's pride.

I am beginning to be able to put things more and more in perspective. I still feel sort of numb for a few days after receiving setbacks, but just try to immerse myself in God's Word and focus on His promises to me. My cancer file (containing all my papers) is covered with Bible texts, and I try to read them while my surgeon is telling me test outcomes. And what a blessing that the surgeon is also a Christian and we all talk very openly about God and the fallen world in which we live and God's plans for restoration. Thank you for your continued prayers and support.

Love, your cousin, and sister in Christ, Helena

Three

The Tests and Operations

When you pass through the waters, I will be with you . . .
When you walk through the fire, you will not be burned.

ISAIAH 43:2

There were times when my life felt like a free fall. Preparing for my third operation was one of them. This surgery was to be a radical step to eliminate my cancer, both pre-cancer and invasive, and would include testing the lymph nodes under my arm to ascertain if those nasty cells had spread into my body.

There were times when I was no longer even trying to be a wife or a mother, but just trying to exist from day-to-day. Times I was just trying to survive. These were times when I would cling to God while the storm buffeted and smashed me against the rocks. I read a quote and realized I was living it: "Sometimes God calms the storm, but sometimes God lets the storm rage and calms His child."[5] The storm was raging. When would God calm His child?

All I could do was to hang on to the Anchor of my soul. Sometimes I felt my grip slipping. How comforting it was, then, to meditate

---

[5] Gould and Clark, *The Amish Nanny*, 342.

on the words of Psalm 73—that God was always with me and wouldn't let me go. I desperately read and reread the reassuring words that He was holding me by His right hand, that He was guiding me with His counsel and that afterward He would take me into Glory. The more time I spent in Scripture, the more I began to become the calmed child. Scriptures like Isaiah 43:1, with its "Do not fear, for I have redeemed you; I have summoned you by name; you are mine" made me feel safe.

My trust in God was increasing as I realized that He would lead me through whatever He led me to. And He was the only One Who could! And why would God do that for me? Isaiah 43:3–4 provides the answer: "For I am the LORD your God, the Holy One of Israel, your Savior . . . you are precious and honored in my sight, and . . . I love you."

The more I meditated on Scripture, the more God's love and presence became something tangible and the more peace I felt. No matter what the future had in store, I knew that His love was all I needed. And that perfect love helped drive out any fears.

Meditation became second nature to me. I didn't just read a portion of the Bible, but I prayed it, and then sat quietly reflecting on it. I began to *seek* opportunities to wait on the LORD, not just wait for opportunities to happen, and I began to safeguard those times as most precious. The more I meditated, the more passages of Scripture seemed to illuminate my mind and heart. I had been reading these same Bible truths for years but now the words were jumping off the pages, words such as the ones I read in Colossians 1:27: "To them God had chosen to make known among the Gentiles the glorious riches of this mystery, which is Christ in you, the hope of glory." This comforting truth was confirmed two chapters later in Colossians 3:3: " . . . Your life is now hidden with Christ in God."

So often I had read that our lives were to be hidden in Christ, but now I felt that that was exactly what was happening to me; I was beginning to really grasp the riches of this mystery! A life hidden in Christ was a life that was not in flux, but a life where God had His grip of covenantal love on me and wasn't going to let go. A life hidden in Christ meant we were in this together, forever. We were inseparable! Reminding myself of this truth when I felt my grip slipping gave me great comfort, knowing that my emotions weren't necessarily truth, but that Scripture was. This dawning realization helped set me on the right course going forward.

A life hidden in Christ was a life that was not in flux, but a life where God had His grip of covenantal love on me.

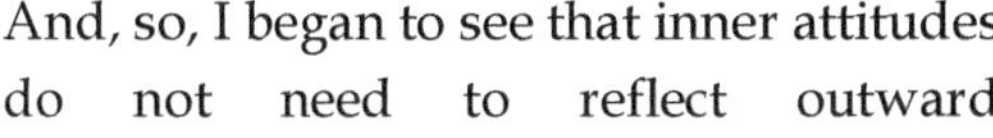

And, so, I began to see that inner attitudes do not need to reflect outward circumstances. That even when outwardly things looked bleak, inwardly, my attitudes, if connected to Christ, could be at their strongest ever—perhaps even stronger than when my outward circumstances are what would be considered good.

I thought of the martyrs who in times past had been burnt at the stake. They sang in the flames! People thought they were crazy. But they weren't. Their outward circumstances did not diminish their scriptural perspective of joy. Their lives were hidden in Christ. And so, although sorrowful, yet they could rejoice (2 Corinthians 6:10).

The apostle Paul urges his hearers in 1 Thessalonians 5:16–18 to "Rejoice always, pray continually, give thanks in all circumstances; for this is God's will for you in Christ Jesus."

Give thanks *for* cancer? No, you don't have to do that. Give thanks *in* cancer? Yes! That's God's will. And with God's help, you can do exactly that. Thank Him for being with you, thank Him for the friendly nurse, for the Christian doctor, thank Him for the prayers of so many as you await your operation, test or treatment, thank Him for the husband by your side. Thank Him that your heart is beating. That the sun is shining. Once you begin to thank God for things, you won't be able to stop—even though you may be in desperate circumstances. Philippians 4:4–7 provides good instruction in this:

> Rejoice in the Lord always. I will say it again: Rejoice! Let your gentleness be evident to all. The Lord is near. Do not be anxious about anything, but in every situation, by prayer and petition, with thanksgiving, present your requests to God. And the peace of God, which transcends all understanding, will guard your hearts and your minds in Christ Jesus.

This is an incredible text. Write it out, memorize it, tuck it in the recesses of your heart and mind, and take it with you to every appointment, into every operating theatre. Don't be anxious! Be thankful. God is near! He has redeemed you through the love of His Son Jesus Christ. You are His. You can have peace because God is in control. You don't need to be in control. You aren't in control. Surrender to Him and bask in His presence. Meditate on His promises to give you peace, the peace that truly surpasses all understanding.

I told myself this over and over as God prepared me for "the dreaded operation." He prepared me in the same way He will prepare you for whatever you are facing. It really was so amazing: I woke up the morning of my operation thinking I didn't want to get out of bed. And here I was, gowned up, waiting for my turn to be wheeled into theatre. My husband was there with me in the waiting bay, and would you believe it? I fell asleep! When the nurse woke me because it was my turn for surgery, she asked unbelievingly, "How can you sleep at a time like this?" I knew the answer. People were praying for me. I was sleeping because I was not anxious. God's call to "fear not" was finding resonance in my soul. I felt overwhelming peace.

While clinging to God's promises and letting them permeate into my soul, I was wheeled into the operating theatre for my third operation in three months, knowing that when I emerged my body would be altered in a way that I could not even allow myself to contemplate a month earlier. I would never be the same again. But I knew something else. The most drastic operation was not being done on my body, but on my soul. It, too, would never be the same.

The next thing I remember was waking up in recovery and the anaesthetist asking me how I felt. I told him the truth: I felt like I was dying! The physical pain was immense. I was so thankful that he put me back under for a while, and this time when I awoke the pain was more manageable. I didn't dare look at my body and decided that it could wait. I just didn't have the emotional fortitude.

My altered body image wasn't at the forefront of my mind at that moment, anyways. The most immediate concern was whether the cancer had spread to the nodes under my arm. If it had, that would open up the possibility that the cancer may be circulating throughout my body. And for that information we had to wait—once again—for results.

The following two weeks were difficult. They were days filled with measuring and emptying drains, checking medication charts, and enduring sleepless nights as I recovered. At times it felt like there was an elephant sitting on my chest and I couldn't breathe, the pressure was so intense. I was sure that if I died, it wouldn't be because of cancer, but it would be death by asphyxiation instead. The nights were the worst, as I would watch the hands on the clock go seemingly backward on their rotation. I was awake, while the rest of the family was asleep. It wouldn't be fair to wake them just to pass the time. But my family in Canada was awake, due to the time difference, and I was so thankful for this provision. I called them often during my recovery and although they couldn't relieve my pain, they could read the Bible and pray with me. This calmed and comforted me tremendously and helped time go by.

One temptation I had to fight during my recovery was that of indulging in self-pity. One day, while half sitting, half lying in my chair (I couldn't lie flat in bed at that time) and listening to my "recovering from operation" playlist of Christian music, I started to feel really sorry for myself. Not often would I allow this feeling to take hold and grow, but this was one occasion where I lapsed. I couldn't take it anymore. The physical pain of recovery coupled with the mental pain of not knowing where this was going to end or how, fuelled further by the emotional pain of having to wait for test results, proved too much for me. I knew Satan was tempting me to "fear" in the face of God's "fear not." I knew that worry was belief gone wrong, but when you are sleep deprived it is so hard to cling to truths, even biblical ones. I started to cry. I knew I needed God's help to combat Satan's temptation.

God provided. In the middle of my self-indulgence, a very close friend stopped by. At first I was surprised God had sent this particular friend as His instrument, because out of my closest friends, she was the least emotional of them. But then I realized God knew exactly what He was doing in sending her. She was precisely who I needed at that moment. She came in, wiped the tears off my face, gave me a hug and said, "Don't cry. It will be all right." The pity party ended as abruptly as it started. Instead of looking inward, I returned to looking upward.

During this time of recuperation I tried to focus on things that I could look forward to. I certainly didn't look forward to my test results and possible treatments, but I did look forward to my oldest sister from Canada visiting! She had never been to Australia before, had never met my family, and now had decided to come and help run our busy household while I recuperated and possibly faced treatment. It was strange how no one seemed to think the next test results would be good news. Almost like we were all resigning ourselves to the fact they wouldn't be. I could see it on everyone's faces; the bad news kept coming and no one was sure if it would stop.

The day of test results came. Two weeks and two days after the operation, it was time to hear if cancer had been banished from my body or if there was more to do battle with. Before we left for the hospital, my husband and I sat down to read the Bible and pray, as we always did before going in. As we prepared for prayer, he looked at me and said, "This morning, I'm not going to pray for the cancer to be gone. I'm going to pray for strength to receive the results God has planned for us." It was another turning point for both of us in this dual axis of God's sovereignty and our responsibility, of knowing God has a plan worked out for us before we are born, but that the prayers of the righteous weave into this plan in a way we can never quite comprehend. It was theology playing out in real time.

We hardly dared look at the receptionist as we entered the surgeon's waiting room and sat down. The words from Isaiah 43:1 that I had been meditating on jumped out at me from my pink cancer folder sitting on my lap: "Do not fear . . . you are Mine."

Do not fear.

When we entered the surgeon's office, we really didn't want him to say anything, which was crazy, because we had waited for these test results for over two agonizing weeks! My cousin Caroline once told me that at least when you don't know the results you can make them anything you want them to be. I guess I had been doing that, but realized I no longer could once the test results were shared. Once the words were spoken, there was no taking them back. And it was time for words to be spoken now.

My doctor opened his mouth and I braced my heart. Then I heard words, but I wasn't sure I heard what I thought I heard.

Did he just say, "Your nodes are clear?"

I looked at my husband. He was as unsure as I was as to what had just been said. We couldn't believe it. It was surreal. It was almost as if having received bad news for so long that we expected more of the same, braced for more of the same. Here our prayers were answered and we found ourselves surprised that God had answered with what we had asked for! We were shocked.

Isn't it strange how when the answer is "no" or "wait" that we don't think our prayers are being heard? Previously, I had prayed for good test outcomes. Instead, the outcomes were disastrous. God did provide an answer, just not the one I wanted or thought was for my good. God's ways are higher than my ways, His thoughts higher than my thoughts, then, as much as now. He wants me to trust Him enough to put my signature at the bottom of the page even when I didn't know what was written on it. God was asking me to trust that the story He was writing for me was a story that would transform me into who He wanted me to be. God is the Author and Perfector of my faith, of my life. Not me.

Sometimes, God answering "no" is exactly what we need. Sometimes, answering "wait" is what's best. And sometimes, often when we least expect it, the Father deems "yes" should be the answer.

I thought of King David. He never realized, as he wrote psalms while running from the deranged King Saul who wanted him dead, how God was using a "wait" answer to accomplish His purposes in David's life. All David knew was that he had been anointed King but wasn't King. Although we don't know for how long, scholars think that David was on the run for about ten years. Ten years of crying out to God for help and protection. Ten years of receiving "wait" answers. But look at the results. David learned total dependence on God while at the same time providing believers with a legacy of irreplaceable Psalms. Can you imagine not having the Psalms in your life?

Maybe the problem doesn't lie with receiving an answer to prayer that we would rather not have had. Maybe the problem is with our short-sightedness. Maybe we need to widen our gaze to what God is accomplishing in the complete story of our lives, not just on one particular page. Maybe we need to widen our gaze even more to what God is doing in His story, of which our story is but one very small and humble part.

Looking back, I didn't know what God had in store for me with my cancer diagnosis. But in hindsight I realize that if God would have given me all "yes" answers to my prayers, I would not have written this book. If it had been all "yes" answers I wouldn't have learned what it meant to wait on God, to depend on Him, and to trust Him completely.

Even though I began to understand these truths about prayer more and more through cancer's experiences, it was wonderful to be able to bask in the glow of God's "yes" answer on this most amazing day. It struck me then how my sister was flying over the ocean at this very moment, flying in trust, not knowing about this good news. I could hardly wait to tell her once she landed.

As my husband and I left the doctor's office, the receptionist gave us a hug and whispered, "God is good." I nodded assent. God is good. Today He was good and my test results were good. But two months ago He was also good, even though my test results weren't. I had learned the lesson that emotions must be centered on truth. Truth not obtained by democratic right, as our western society has led us to believe. Truth not based on our emotions, as our emotions would have us believe. Truth based on one source and one source alone: the Word of God. And that Word reveals the same message over and over about God, and that is that God is good. God was good when my test results were good. God was good when my test results weren't good. God is simply good.

Emotions must be centered on truth, truth based on the Word of God, truth that tells us God is good even when test results aren't.

It was time to rejoice and celebrate! In our excitement, we drove straight to our children's school to share the incredible news—the cancer had not spread! But even while saying these words, the good news still felt quite surreal. Was it really true? But slowly, over time, we all let ourselves begin to absorb the reality that there was no more evidence of disease.

A month later, after a final visit with the surgeon, we said our goodbyes to my medical team. A few months after that, to mark our twentieth wedding anniversary, we celebrated once again on a sunset boat cruise around Bunbury's beautiful harbor along with those who had walked through cancer's journey with us. It was a special evening commemorating God's goodness and love toward us.

The cancer was gone! I had come full circle. I had passed through the waters, the rivers, and the fire and had emerged on the other side. God had made a way in the wilderness and streams in the wasteland. Now, it was time to resume my life. It was time to get back to normal.

Hello Helena . . .

So thankful to read the news that the surgery is completed and you are back at home. What a relief to have this behind you, and you can move on to the next step of this journey. One day at a time the Lord will lead you and I pray for strength and healing, that you may be up and about soon. Please don't overdo yourself (which is easy to do because you just want to be back to normal, and because you are a mother in a busy household) but force yourself to rest, rest, rest!!! I had a hard time with this, so I suspect you might as well.

Well, I am still praying daily for you all, and you have been in my thoughts a lot these past days. I guess because I've been down your road, I feel so much more connected to you. I want to do all I can for you, but realize the distance between us makes this difficult. Please let me know if you have any questions I might answer. I am reading a very good book about a pastor who went through cancer . . . it's called "My God is True!" by Paul D. Wolfe. I highly recommend it. This man was twenty-eight and newly married, studying to be a minister when he was diagnosed with cancer. His spiritual insights are so powerful, it has brought me so much peace and joy to read. If you can't find it there I will try to mail it to you, or send it with someone going your way. Take care and God Bless!

Love, Caroline

Hi Caroline,

Thank you for taking the time to write an email before leaving for your holiday. I love reading your emails because I know you have walked in my shoes and understand the emotional, spiritual, and physical battle that cancer is.

Recuperation is harder than I thought it would be; sleeping isn't working very well and some of the meds I am on are making me quite nauseous, so not being able to keep down much food at the moment, which just makes me weaker. But I'm so glad the operation is behind me. Recovery didn't go so well; apparently they had to knock me out again (Andrew told me this; it's all hazy to me) to get my pain under control. Anyways, I'm home with four drains and it feels like an elephant's sitting on my chest!! We are so thankful that they managed to find the sentinals so that they didn't have to do an axillary clearance. I'm already trying to do my exercises to prevent any shoulder/arm stiffness. I'm hoping on Sunday to lose two of the four drains.

I really have been carried by God through this time and even though I am very sad about my loss, I'm not as overwhelmed by it as I thought I might be. Andrew's been an amazing support, he's got my medications all charted out, empties and measures my drains and makes me feel beautiful even though I feel anything but.

Caroline, I just want to say again how much I appreciate you being one of my blessings on this road. Thanks for being my sister in Christ.

Love, Helena

Four

The Circle

And let us run with perseverance the race marked out for us.

HEBREWS 12:1

I had been waiting a long time for today.

Today was to be the day that I put cancer behind me for good and return to my normal life.

It had been a year and a half since receiving the amazing news that there was no remaining evidence of disease left. Now, I was facing one last hurdle—surgery to restore my body to what it had once been before the ravages of cancer. Surgery that would help me to feel whole and beautiful once again. Surgery to close the circle and end this unpleasant interlude in my life.

I had prayed for the closure this operation represented: wanting it and needing it. Now I was so close! My life was about to return to normal. One more operation and we could move on from the events of the past two years. I could return to being one more normal Mom doing normal Mom things: soccer practice and music lesson runs, buying groceries, washing endless loads of laundry, reading home readers, doing spelling lists, and a million and one other mundane, beautiful things. Why had I never realized before what blessings these everyday events were? How in their normalcy they were anything but normal? And now they were close once again—within reach!

I knew it wasn't going to be plain sailing. This was to be a massive operation to fix up my battered body. It would be a long, hard recovery. But I felt ready. I had been on the waitlist for a year, prepared myself for a year, and it was finally time. I was sure it was the means to my end: the closure I so craved.

The morning of the operation found my thoughts confident and bold. "Bring it on," I thought. But as I made last-minute preparations, my nervousness ramped up. With every minute that brought me closer to the operating theatre, my confidence dissipated. I had been busy memorizing Psalm 62 over the past week and tried to combat my unease by using the Psalm to anchor my thoughts as the time for surgery drew ever nearer: "Truly He is my rock and my salvation; He is my fortress, I will never be shaken" (Psalm 62:2).

The day-long surgery was over very quickly for me, in my state of unconsciousness. I'm sure it felt much longer for my surgeons. For them, it was an arduous undertaking. As I awoke in recovery, I knew I wouldn't make it without God's strength. I suppose you can prepare yourself for a surgery such as this by reading others' accounts of their recuperations, but really, until you've gone through it, you just don't know what it would be like. Maybe that's for the best.

But here I was—on the other side. It was extremely difficult, very tiring, and it took about a day before I realized that I would actually survive. Each day seemed like I was running a marathon as goals changed from simply focusing my eyes, to sitting up in bed, to the luxury of having a shower.

Every day seemed an eternity, but finally after five days I was allowed to go home. As I waited for my sweet family to come and return me to my old life, I wrote a poem which I entitled, *Closed*

Circle. In it I poured out my emotions, all my accumulated experiences and concluded in thanksgiving to God. I thought my refining was done, and that the circle could now close and I could return to my old life. It was a poem that I would not get to share. Not as it stood.

In hindsight, I should have known. Known something was up, known that my surgeon didn't seem thrilled even though the operation had been so successful. If I didn't know that something was amiss while in hospital, I definitely should have known when I returned a week later to have my dressings checked. Here I was being asked to put on a gown only to be told to change back into my clothes and wait in my surgeon's office. But, wait, he wasn't even in today, so, what exactly was going on? Why don't you just check my dressings and let me go home? I had a life to get back to—you remember, the normal one!

My husband and I had driven in that morning in a buoyant, jubilant mood. I was feeling better, the results were more than we could have hoped for, and we had sung and laughed all the way to the hospital.

So, when my surgeon walked through his office door, I pushed back the bothersome thoughts that had begun to assault my brain. I tried to return to the jubilant mood of the drive in and remember that this was my last hospital date for the foreseeable future. Finally, this cancer thing was over. The circle was oh so close to closing.

But then we looked at his face. Whereas we were jubilant, he was not. He was serious. He stood before us and solemnly asked us to sit down. I still remember what I was wearing, the couch we sat down on. I remember every detail, like I was watching it from out of my body. I remember seeing my surgeon's expression and realizing something was very wrong. The slow-motion feeling returning. I knew I had to keep him from talking. But before I could say, "Stop!", he started. I didn't know what he was going to say, but I knew with utmost certainty I didn't want him to say it.

I wanted everything to pause, to rewind this day, to go back to how I was feeling an hour ago.

But I couldn't. I didn't control time. I didn't control circumstance. There was only One who did that. And He had called this day into being. Had called this situation into being. Had called this moment into being. Nothing about today was random. God was here. That much I knew.

So, my surgeon's words came. Spoken and free. Not retractable by their very existence. He said that while operating he had come across something unexpected: an enlarged and red lymph node in my central mammary chain. It was discovered by him almost by accident as a result of having to move a rib. And there it was. Behind this rib. Previously undetected because it was in a place it shouldn't be. Cancer doesn't spread that way. That's what the medical world had us believing, anyway. That's not its normal escape route into the body—the lymph nodes under my arm were. *And those lymph nodes had been clear.* So, I was supposed to be okay!

I wanted everything to pause, to rewind this day, to go back to how I was feeling an hour ago.

And, yet, there it was, discovered in a place where it shouldn't have been. Removed, and sent to pathology for testing.

And now, we were here. The pathology results were here. The verdict was here. I heard the words ricochet back and forth in my head. "The results came back cancerous."

Here we go again.

I felt like I had been broadsided. With everything I had learned about this disease, this possibility hadn't ever surfaced.

How could this be?

All feelings of incredible happiness and closure we had felt earlier that morning instantly disappeared and were replaced by paralyzing numbness.

I wanted to run, but couldn't move and didn't know where I could run to anyways. I cried out to God in my soul, but no words would form in my mind. I went into autopilot, asking for a copy of the pathology report, not believing it until I saw the words on paper. I was still holding out for that dream of closure by its slimmest thread. But words kept coming; they wouldn't stop. Words on the report, verifying the verbal. Words from my mouth, telling my husband it would be okay, we've been here before. Words from my surgeon, advising me to go to the cancer wing of the hospital to talk about treatment. No discharge. No closure. Treatment. That was to be my next chapter. But wait! Chapter? There wasn't supposed to be a next chapter. The circle was supposed to close!

I wished for light in the darkness. Please, LORD, some small glimmer? Then I heard my doctor speak:

"This discovery may just have saved your life."

Thankfulness in adversity, beauty in brokenness. It was all here, co-mingled with the circle's cavernous opening. There was more to learn, more to live, more to understand, more to be refined. I couldn't close any circles, because I wasn't in charge. Why would I want to be, anyway? Why did I crave my old normal, when the whole point was to change my normal, to change me, to purify me? Why did I want to go back to my old creation, when the new was being forged? Didn't I realize what this was about? Was I really so slow to learn and understand?

Thankfulness in adversity, beauty in brokenness – it was all here.

I thought about the biblical allegory of running the race (1 Corinthians 9:24–27). Sometimes you think you can compete without preparation, but if you really want that prize you need strict training. I was now in strict training. It was hard, painful work; it was gruelling. This was no leisurely jog in the park. I was competing in the marathon of my life to receive the crown that would last forever! I could almost sense the spiritual sweat beading on my soul. And so I prayed, no longer for closure, but for strength and endurance. The dawning of acceptance of God's will in my life, and the life of my family, began to surface in my consciousness.

My husband was still in shock. I didn't know what to say to him. All the words had been spoken. The Word had spoken. There was nothing left to utter. It was time to move forward. To leave the office and cross the hospital to the cancer wing. There, a radiation oncologist was waiting to make plans with us. Different plans than we had planned. Plans for radiation. Possibly plans for chemotherapy. Plans that made me wonder if the circle would ever close, and whether that was maybe the point of this all. Almost like beauty of the soul could only emerge through brokenness of the spirit, of the will, of the control, of the self-sufficiency, of the independence. The race had to be finished, the restoration of my soul completed.

There was to be no closure in a broken world—only a gradual shift toward one, with a foretaste of a future beauty already found in the broken, a foretaste that left a yearning for more. A foretaste that God promised would become a full reality when the circle would close in the fullness of time. Then there would be beauty, not in brokenness, but in perfection.

God was continuing to work with me—would He ever finish? How much refining was enough? Yet even though the second blow was so much harder because I knew what this diagnosis meant—I was, after all, no longer clueless to the world of cancer—yet it was softer because I also knew what God's promises meant, and knew I would experience the surety of His presence throughout this second round.

This unbelievable turn of events was no accident, no random occurrence. Nothing with God ever is or was. But even while thankful that my cancer was providentially discovered when by all accounts it should not have been, our thankfulness was tinged with devastation and pain. Why did it drain to the central mammary nodes in the first place? In the confusion, I knew there was only one thing I could do: put my hand in His and go forward in His strength.

So forward into the unknown I would go with the God I was getting to know more and more. God was teaching me that strength wasn't to be found in myself, but that my strength lay entirely in my weakness and dependence on Him. My hands were empty.

It was time to return to the track and keep running for the prize. There was no time to take a breather. Two days later saw us back in the hospital for a bone scan to check if cancer had spread there. That same afternoon I had a CT[6] scan to check my soft tissue for signs of invasion. Time was of the essence, now. The enemy needed to be located, and fast. This was an aggressive cancer and needed to be found, confronted, and, to preserve my life, eradicated.

My husband and I realized full well that these test outcomes would be game-changers. If the cancer had spread outside the nodes, any treatment would be life-extending, not life-preserving. But if it was contained, treatment could be curative.

Apart from my cousin Caroline, no one knew about this second diagnosis, no one knew that we were waiting for life-altering news. We had made the choice to wait with telling anyone until our children's exams were over. Wanted to wait so we could enjoy the special Sunday where our firstborn son stood ready to commit his life to God in response to God's promises made to him many years ago at his baptism. And so, we waited. It seemed strange that no one knew—no one, except Someone. And so, we relinquished our hearts to Him: our Lord and Savior, Jesus Christ.

---

[6] Computed Tomography.

We surrendered our hearts to the One who knew how agonizing waiting was. The One who simply knew.

Three days later, on Friday afternoon, as I sat on my back deck overlooking the beautiful sun-kissed hills, I rang to obtain the results of the scans. They showed no evidence of cancer. There were some indeterminate findings relating to my central mammary nodes and a small patch on my lung, but the rest of my body showed no signs of disease.

This was *unbelievable* and very good news!

I could hardly take it in.

Because of the inconclusiveness of the nodes and nodule, I was asked to return the following week for a PET[7] scan and an ultrasound with biopsy. Time would show these results to also be inconclusive. I wasn't sure if inconclusive was good news or bad. I didn't know how to feel. Was I to be relieved because the cancer wasn't in my bones or soft tissue? Or should I be worrying if there was more cancer in my central mammary chain or in my lung?

I felt I was on a roller-coaster ride of extremes. Good outcomes, bad outcomes, inconclusive outcomes—all at the same time. I began to realize that results didn't give concrete answers, they didn't give certainty. Only God is certain and gave certainty.

God is never indeterminate. God's actions are never inconclusive. I had to turn to Him. My answers needed to be found in His Word. And there I read that I was to keep running this race with perseverance. Running into a future I didn't know, but a future that He knew and was in control of.

So, in His strength, I would run. In His strength I would jump hurdles along the way. I would keep my eyes on my Pioneer and Perfector. And I would bear my cross and follow Him for the joy set before me as I continued to endure the strict training that

---

[7] Positron Emission Tomography.

would help me run the race of my life. And I would not grow weary and lose heart.

Dear Caroline,

Thank you for sharing the Corrie ten Boom quotes. I have printed them out and will take it to my back deck where I am spending some time at the moment with God trying to anchor myself in Him, my Rock, because I tell you (and you already know this!) that this is incredibly hard. We had the most beautiful day with our son's profession of faith yesterday, with an amazing sermon about running the race. Well, not only was it a message for him but a message for his mother too! We told my husband's parents yesterday and tomorrow my brother is going to my Mom and Dad's and telling them. I just can't tell them myself. Throughout the week I'll tell my siblings and then on Thursday night (once all their exams are finished) we hope to tell the children, God willing.

I think the uncertainly of my prognosis, along with the oncologist's reluctance to stage me, is giving me anxiety and I am really going to try to release that all to God so am taking this week off from appointments, etc to first get my spiritual side sorted. Then and only then can we begin to make our way through the maze of test results, information, and planning sessions. Psalm 91 still calms my soul and I am currently trying to memorize Psalm 57: "Have mercy on me, my God, have mercy on me, for in You I take refuge. I will take refuge in the shadow of Your wings until the disaster has passed." Be assured we continue to hold you in our prayers as we realize full well the road you are travelling is not easy. Hope your blood test went well and that you don't have to wait too long for results . . . you may even have yours back before mine.

With love, Helena

Dear Helena,

Thinking about you all day today . . . still hard to absorb this news. Just wondering how your tests went today. You did say you were getting your PET today? Hope it went well, I guess you won't know results for a few days. Waiting is not nice, but I never minded thinking no news is better than bad news.

My bloodwork did not have good results . . . both tumour markers are up, so thinking my onc will have me changing medicines Usually only one was above normal, but now the c125 has jumped up as well. That one marks the protein in the blood.

Well, dear cousin, it seems we are both in the same boat of uncertainty. Thankfully our Captain is in charge and we can let Him direct our paths.

Lots of love and hugs to you . . . Caroline 

Five

The Chemotherapy

Rejoice always, pray continually, give thanks in all circumstances.

1 THESSALONIANS 5:16–18

At times, time did seem to stop. But, of course, it didn't really. Nearly two months had passed since my shocking second cancer diagnosis and, in the meantime, a new year had begun. It's really quite amazing how cancer alters the way you view and celebrate events—birthdays, anniversaries, the changing of the year. I found myself becoming much more reflective, much more thankful. I no longer assumed that one year would simply turn into another. The refining my Refiner was doing was transforming my soul.

But it wasn't all beautiful. Satan had used the weeks following my unexpected recurrence to attack. It was most palpable during the days right after we heard the devastating news. Waiting to tell family and friends came at the cost of not having myriads of prayers to surround me. How could people pray when they didn't know? And yet, I desperately needed those prayers! Satan knew it; I knew it.

Those had been hard days. Although it had been somewhat of a relief to finally tell the children that my cancer had returned, it was still heart-wrenchingly difficult. Seeing them absorb the unabsorbable, seeing them lose faith in the medical system that had a year ago given me the all clear, seeing them wonder why God would first give healing only to take it away again caused me and them untold pain.

They wondered how the statistics could have been so wrong. I had been wondering the same thing, too, actually, and in my wondering wondered whether I had inadvertently put my trust in statistics. The more I thought about this the more the truth emerged that I wasn't a random statistic whose name appeared in a medical study journal. I was a covenant child of God and was His statistic! When the rule book of cancer was broken and trod upon, it was because God was doing the breaking and treading. Test results were God's results. Statistics could be wrong or they could be right, depending on what God determined. Because He is LORD of statistics!

But these lessons weren't easy to learn. Not being able to stand my children's pain was my weak point, and Satan knew it and used it. For the first time I could remember, doubts assaulted me: doubts as to where this was going, and when and how it would end. Hadn't I learned enough? Did things really need to be taken to this point? Couldn't the children be spared? Surely it would've been easier to not have healed me in the first place! My prayers during this time often became soul outpourings as I begged God to stop Satan from tormenting me. I felt like I was on a spiritual roller-coaster ride—one day strong in faith and trust, the next, filled with uncertainty and doubt. My prayers reflected this, often ending with the words of Mark 9:24: "I do believe; help me overcome my unbelief!"

Not being able to stand my children's pain was my weak point, and Satan knew it and used it.

It was also a most difficult time because of the decision making that needed to happen. Although the cancer wasn't in my bones or soft tissue, there were still the indeterminate findings in my central mammary chain and lung. That, and also the possibility of stray cancer cells, meant treatment was necessary. But how drastically do we treat this cancer? Do we wait and see, or start immediately? What is the right balance between God's sovereign plan for my life, and my responsibility in determining treatment plans? I trusted God, but also knew I had to use His good gifts of medicine for my wellbeing. Where was the line? What if some saw the line here and others saw the line there? Did I trust too much in medicine and not enough in God? This was tricky territory and required much prayer and wisdom. Compounding this situation, my husband and I discovered our views on where responsibility and sovereignty met were not quite aligned. Up until now we had agreed upon everything. This brought its own set of temptations.

But then, slowly, steadily, things began to change. Maybe it was the prayers of the saints battering God's throne room once again, now that the saints knew. Maybe the angels were gaining ground in the spiritual warfare being undertaken on my soul. Whatever was happening, I began to feel different and the peace surpassing all understanding brought balm to my soul once again. The Light was shining and the darkness was being dispelled. I felt that Satan had been dealt a blow! Tough decisions were made. Treatment was agreed upon and organized.

And so, a week before Christmas, I sat in a place I never thought I would sit: the chemotherapy chair. I felt emotional, but peaceful. And then provision came from my Provider: next to my cubicle a woman set up her harp and played beautiful Christmas carols, carols that reminded me that Jesus Christ came into this world for me, died for me, rose for me, had been crowned King and was preparing a place for me to live together with Him. How could things not turn out for the best?

It's a very strange feeling having poison pumping through your veins in order to kill rebellious cancer cells. Rebellious, because these cells weren't doing what they were originally created to do before the fall into sin. It was the battle of good versus evil being played out right in my body! Cancer attacks God's beautiful creation in an attempt to mar it. Cells designed to listen to their nuclei and do specific jobs and reproduce normally were instead causing havoc. And they wanted to spread their havoc! And yet, God is King over body and soul and weaves this rebellion into His divine purposes.

Chemotherapy wasn't too bad, I thought to myself a week later on Christmas day. I still managed to go to church, cook Christmas turkey on the barbecue and have friends over, although I needed a little rest on the couch afterward. I had been confident I could handle treatment. I was mentally strong and physically in good shape. The warning signs should've begun to register, but they hadn't; warning signs that I was beginning to depend on my own strength, my own resilience. But this all changed when my hair started falling out, two days before a new year began.

I thought I was prepared for this day, but I hadn't been prepared. Not even close.

I thought I was prepared for this day. The wig was ready to go. I had told myself it was only hair, but I hadn't been prepared. Not even close. In retrospect, I realized that it had been so very difficult to lose my hair because this was another blow to my identity as a woman. I had lost so much already. Now I would lose my long dark hair too? When would the losses end? When would this attack on God's creation of the female body end?

I called two of my friends and they came over to shave the rest of my hair off, so that I no longer needed to endure it coming out in clumps all over my pillow. They cried with me. They laughed with me. They had wine and cheese on my back deck with me.

They were the hands and feet of God's love to me. Once again, God had led me through what He led me to.

And now a new year had begun. What would its days hold? Only God knew.

Three weeks after my first treatment, I was back for my second infusion. This concoction of toxins, injected by medical staff in their special protective suits, went against the grain. If they had to protect themselves from being *around* this poison, what about my body having it injected *into* its very lifeblood? In this instance there seemed to be no other way than to fight evil with evil.

As I sat in the chemo chair once again, I thought about my cousins Nellie and Caroline, both fighting their own battles with cancer at this very same moment in time, both encouraging mentors to me, both provisions from the LORD for my journey. It was surreal, to say the least, that all three of us cousins were in this together, across the oceans from one another. It was amazing grace that all of us were at peace with God and could support one another in our relationships with Him, encouraging one another to hold fast and trust God's plans for our lives.

But God gave even more. During my second treatment, my surgeon's receptionist, who, unbeknownst to me, now worked in the chemo ward, walked by. She was rather surprised to see me in the chair as she hadn't known about my second diagnosis. It was emotional to see each other again almost two years later, and I confided to her that I had two cousins who had cancer who weren't doing well physically and I wasn't sure which way things would go for them. I confessed I was fearful that since their earthly prognosis wasn't looking good, perhaps mine wouldn't go well either. I'll never forget what she said to me: "God's story for each of them is different to His story for you." Yes, genetics might say otherwise, but the Bible confirms the truth of her words. So does my life. God has a divine design for all who belong to Him, and uses unique circumstances to mold and shape His children, to sanctify them, and to ensure that His plans for them are accomplished, using the means He deems best to complete what He has started in their lives.

Three weeks later I was back in hospital for round three. This was a turning point for me in many ways, and is probably best expressed in sharing what I wrote in an email to my closest family:

> Third chemo
>
> On Tuesday morning I met with my medical oncologist and got the go ahead for my third chemo treatment even though my white blood cell count was just below the cutoff. I was expecting a low count as I have been noticing other side effects beginning to surface—the tiredness, the chemo burn, and some forgetfulness. It's doing its job and it's a job that has to be done, but I am so thankful it is nearly over. I'm reading a book right now called *The Hardest Peace* by Kara Tippetts. She writes this: "Chemo brings silence. A deafening silence to just get through each moment. Silence to my robust personality, silence to my children, my friends, my love. Painful, grievous silence where there had once been constant, loving chatter."[8]
>
> And Kara is right in some ways. Sometimes I just want to withdraw, especially the day before treatment and the week after. This time, the day before chemo saw me feeling like Jonah, wanting to find a ship and sail away. Instead, my good friend drove me to the hospital and I found flowers waiting there along with a note of encouragement from another good friend. God's provision once again.
>
> I sense a change occurring in my soul. And I think that's the point of God's refining hand in my life. John Keats once wrote: "Do you not see how necessary a World of Pains and troubles is to school an Intelligence and make it a soul?"[9] And yet, through the hard moments, God gives me a deep sense of His presence, and my blessings come into a sharper focus. I feel a deep sense of being blessed as His child, of being blessed with my godly and wonderful husband and six beautiful children. I'm enjoying the little moments of life so much more—reading

[8] Tippetts, *The Hardest Peace*, 89.

[9] Keats, *Letters of John Keats*, 256.

> a story with my youngest and seeing him sound out the words; talking with my preteener about middle school; looking at and paying attention to my younger daughter's varied pets; having coffee with my two oldest, and listening to every, and I mean every, word of my second youngest's devotional "sermons." I'm no longer rushing these moments, but absorbing them, pondering them, and treasuring them.
>
> I also sense a change in my trust in God. My theology was always there as a strong foundation. And I believed. And I trusted. And I had a strong, loving relationship with Him. But this is rubber hitting the road theology, this is God's sovereignty up close and personal in my very own life. And not only my life, but also the lives of all who love me. Am I going to trust God 95 percent? Or 100 percent? How painful would that last 5 percent be?
>
> Perhaps some of you reading this are wondering if I am being gloomy or perhaps not hopeful of the future. Nothing can be further from the truth. We are fighting this battle with everything we have and will continue to do so. But I think I would be missing God's point if I didn't stop and reflect on what this is all about. Is it about how long we live or how we live? Cancer brings me perspective and I am enjoying that along with a deeper intimacy with God, my husband and children, and also you, my family. Would I want to wish it on anyone? Absolutely not. Would I say I wish it had never happened? I'm no longer sure. I want to be a woman who is beautiful in God's eyes. And maybe I need to suffer in order to become this beautiful.

I wonder if my family, after reading my email, thought that the chemotherapy was affecting more than just my cancer. Perhaps it was killing my brain cells as well! It seemed I wasn't always relating to people anymore the way I used to—that I was coming across very intense. But it was an intense time. And this intensity made it hard to relate to others at times. This brought a loneliness of its own as I traversed waters that others hadn't, while experiencing blessings that were unique.

It was after this third chemo treatment that my body began to display some serious effects. Chemo burn appeared on my arm, my face looked ashen, and I felt exhausted. The good news was that I only had one more treatment to go. The bad news was I wasn't sure if I could do one more.

Then, as if there wasn't enough happening, news from my cousin Nellie's daughter arrived. Nellie had died. Charles Spurgeon would say of this moment that a fresh star had lit up the celestial firmament with an added splendor and that a new voice was heard in the choir of the redeemed.[10] I don't doubt it.

Nellie's death left me with mixed feelings. I was relieved her suffering was over and was thankful for the encouragement and example she had been to me. But it was strange to realize she was no longer on this earth. I would sorely miss her! Now, there was only Caroline and me left dealing with this dreaded disease called cancer. And Caroline, while growing stronger in faith, seemed to be growing weaker in body. There seemed to be a correlation between the two: the more her physical state deteriorated, the more her faith flourished! It was amazing to behold—a fast-tracked transformation going on before my eyes! Caroline was demonstrating with her very life what it meant to rejoice in all circumstances and this reality was made possible by her total dependence and trust in God's plans and promises.

The end of the Australian long, hot summer brought me to what was to be the last lap in my chemo marathon. I was jubilant that this was to be my final time in the chair. Added to that, I was excited about picking up my brother and his wife from the airport the very next day. I had so much to look forward to!

My three friends brought me to this last treatment, determined to make me laugh and smile throughout—so much so that one of them was warned that she would need to leave if she didn't quiet down! We celebrated afterward with champagne at the beach. My

[10] Spurgeon, "Why the Heavenly Robes are White," Sermon 1316.

diary excerpt gives this insight into the changes God continued to work in me:

> Today was my last chemo treatment. My whites were much better than round three so I was good to go. After meeting with my oncologist I went with my three friends to the chemo ward. After three foiled attempts to get a blood vessel, I think we were all ready to bolt—even the nurse! But we got there in the end and the poison was all safely injected two hours later. I love the beauty that exists in the spectrum of suffering, strange as that sounds. Sometimes I think there's more beauty—certainly more depth—than exists on the carefree side of life. My longings to go back to the other side are abating while my thankfulness for the enrichment of my life on the level of suffering increases. How can this be? God is working in mysterious ways.

I was so grateful for my three friends. They tried to understand, and at times I truly think they did. All uniquely different, they were godly and loyal, and the three of them together were exactly the gift I needed for this morning's journey. They had been by my side through it all, even though at times it was very confronting.

I felt thankful for many things. I was thankful to God for being my all-in-all. Thankful that just last night my struggling son had opened up to me about his fears of the chemo not working, his fears of me dying. But, above all, I was thankful that in spite of his fears, this son was no longer angry with God.

Still, the days following this last treatment continued to be a roller-coaster ride of highs and lows and everything in between. Despite chemo's completion, the accumulated treatments continued to take their toll on my body. My face went from looking ashen to looking like I was wearing a death mask. All the "you look beautiful, you're handling things so well" comments abruptly came to an end. Things were getting tough and we knew it.

So here I was, post-chemo, physically weak, but, by God's grace, gaining in spiritual strength. The changes I noticed in Caroline were now changes I was noticing in me! It was quite exciting in a strange sort of way. I had often pondered Hebrews 2:10 where it explains that Christ through suffering learned perfect obedience. Now I was being shown clearly how Christ knows suffering like no other person ever will. My suffering would never be anything near what He endured because He endured it for me. This realization filled me with gratitude.

Refining was hard, but through the hardness of it all I liked the changes in me, the understanding of purpose it was illuminating in me. I began cherishing my blessings and pondering things in my heart in a way I had never done before. Not that I hadn't counted my blessings or thought about God when I was healthy—not at all. But it was different now. Maybe it was because I was forced to slow down and, as a result, savoured my relationship with God and also with others so much more. I loved that! And so, even though cancer is something I would never have asked for or would never wish on anyone, I was beginning to think that perhaps, just perhaps, it was something I would not want to give back. The beauty I was discovering in the brokenness was just too special.

Even though I was quite ill, I was resolute in my plans to make the two hour drive to Perth in order to pick up my brother and sister-in-law from the airport the day after my last chemo treatment. I stopped in at my mother-in-law on the way, who, when she saw how unwell I was, pleaded with me to allow her to go instead. But there was no way I was going to miss this moment for anything.

Welcoming my Canadian brother and his wife on Australian soil was amazing. My family back in Canada had been such a support to me, but to have my brother physically present, representing them, was euphoric. I braced myself for the shocked reaction I thought my appearance would trigger—they hadn't seen any of the declines the recent months of operations and treatments had brought. But if my brother and his wife felt shocked, they hid it admirably well. There was not one cringe in sight! They looked at me like I was the most beautiful woman on the planet. I was overjoyed. What a special day, a day where I could almost forget all about cancer.

However, this was to be a rather short hiatus. The very next day saw us meeting with the radiation oncologist to plan the radiation schedule, beginning within the month. Again, the tension between God's sovereignty and man's responsibility surfaced and needed to be worked through. It was helpful to have my brother and his wife in on the conversation this time around. The dilemmas surrounding our diverging understanding on this subject continued to be an area where Satan tried to gain entry, tried to create disunity between my husband and I. Thankfully, our marriage was not a twofold, but a threefold cord, with God providing the strength that enabled protection of this vital union.

During these few weeks of transitioning between chemo and radiation, news came that my dear cousin Caroline was getting much weaker. She had been in palliative care for almost two months and our frequent emails back and forth showed God was preparing her to receive her crown of glory. I desperately wanted to be there to say, "until we meet again," but it was impossible. My brother and his wife felt the same, as they, too, had a close relationship with Caroline.

With her never far from my thoughts, I commenced planning for the next stage of my treatment. The oncologist decided to do a PET scan before radiation instead of after, as had originally been planned. This meant that we would find out whether the chemotherapy had been successful in eradicating cancer cells before we even began radiation.

We were definitely not ready for this change of tactics, and only having the weekend to adjust and prepare ourselves spiritually and emotionally seemed impossible. We wrote this email to our family and close friends:

> This hasn't given us long to prepare spiritually and emotionally for the possible results of this test, so we write this email asking you to bring this in prayer before our Father's

throne. The last chemo session was especially difficult on Helena's body, with its effects still felt now, and we ask God that what she has gone through enduring treatment will not be in vain. We entreat the Great Physician for healing of Helena's body from cancer so that she can continue on with us longer here on earth. We pray for strength, that whatever Tuesday's results may or may not be, that God will give us and our children courage and complete trust in Him.

Before I had time to contemplate things further, there was more news. (News just kept coming!) This news was news I had been expecting. But it was still painful news. My dear cousin Caroline, whom I loved like a sister, had been promoted to eternal life. Of all three cousins, only I remained. I felt such a range of conflicting emotions: joy, that she could now see her Savior face-to-Face and that all her tests, waiting, fighting, and running were over. Thankfulness, for all she had meant to so many people and for the godly mentor and encourager she could be to me. And deep, profound sadness, that I could no longer speak with her or see her this side of heaven.

Still, there was another feeling, this one taking me by surprise. I felt a hint of jealousy that for Caroline it was all over. For me it wasn't. There was more uncertainty, more treatments, more tests, and more of everything for me. For Caroline there was only more joy, more healing, more basking in the glory of Christ.

One last emotion I experienced was that of survivor guilt. This had plagued me before and would plague me again. I was alive while my two cousins weren't. I knew that was God's decision. Caroline and Nellie had known that too. But at times, I still felt guilty that I was—so far—chosen to live.

The day of Caroline's funeral was the same day as my PET scan; the same day I would hear whether chemotherapy had been successful. I got up early to watch the live streaming of the funeral but couldn't watch it all as it was time to leave for the hospital. Grabbing my Bible, my devotion book, and my prayer journal I jumped in the car with my husband, brother, and sister-in-law to make the familiar two-hour trek from country to city. The drive up was contemplatively quiet. *Caroline's funeral is today. My test is today.* I think we all realized the gravity of the moment.

On the drive in, I reflected on the words of Psalm 63:7–8: "Because You are my help I sing in the shadow of Your wings. I cling to You; Your right hand upholds me." I wrote this text on my hand and so took these words of promise with me into the PET scan room. And God delivered. I don't think I ever felt so peaceful. The room seemed so bright, angel bright, almost. Something had happened as I meditated on Psalm 63. God had brought me to a place of peace where results seemingly no longer mattered. All that mattered was being in His presence. I was receiving a little foretaste of what living with God in eternity could be like.

Before I could bask for too long in my spiritual euphoria, the PET scan was done and I was dressed and waiting to meet with the doctor for the results. I tried to read the expression on her face as she approached, but couldn't. I asked if I could get my husband before she communicated the outcome, an outcome that would determine so much of what lay ahead.

I went back to the waiting room and, after giving my brother and his wife a hug and asking them to pray (I don't think they had stopped!), my husband and I returned and heard the doctor's words: *"The internal mammary chain nodes have responded to the treatment!"* We were shocked! All that chemo had actually been worth it. God had used it to prolong my life. The relief was tangible, the news amazing, and the thanksgiving overflowing. I tried to remind myself that God would still have been good if the news hadn't been good. But it was oh so sweet to have the combination of God being good *and* the news being good!

Nevertheless, I was a seasoned veteran by this time. I knew that cancer was a cruel oppressor. I knew that there were sure to be twists and turns around the corner. I knew I still needed to endure radiation to target lurking cancer cells that remained. I knew that "no evidence of disease" (NED) didn't mean that every last cancer cell was gone.

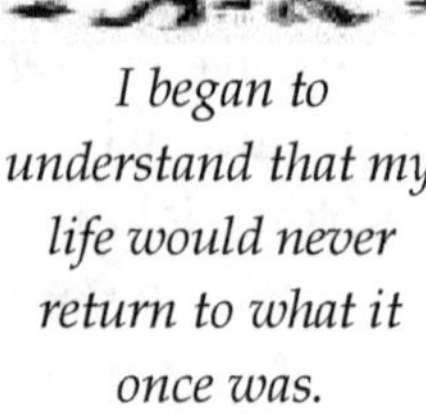

I began to understand that my life would never return to what it once was.

I began to understand that my life would never—could never—return to what it once was. The circle that I had wanted to close so I could go back would never close this side of heaven. Instead, God was bringing about a longing for what lay ahead—an eternal future I now had a sharper awareness of. And so, I no longer craved closure like I once had. The only closure I now desired lay up ahead and would happen when the time—God's time—had fully come. Augustine was right when he once prayed: "Thou madest us for Thyself, and our heart is restless, until it repose in Thee."[11]

The grace of my Lord Jesus Christ was with me. I had my hope of salvation and the promise of what awaited. Time with God had brought me to the place where I could be thankful and rejoice in all circumstances—through bad results, and now good.

---

[11] Augustine of Hippo, *The Confessions of St. Augustine*, Chapter 1.

Dear Caroline . . . a parting gift

I made a friend a few years ago
It was someone I had always known
Our fathers brothers, mothers sisters too
We are truly cousins through and through

Because of age we weren't in each other's lives
But circumstance would change and strengthen the ties
Our all faithful God was about to show
His plan for our days and the way we would go

Cancer took us by storm, would things ever be the same?
Yours diagnosed first and five months later my news came
As you reached out to comfort and encourage me
I realized what a blessing you would always be

We both learned the meaning of real surrender
As our friendship grew, our conversations more tender
The answers, although not always easily found,
Were sought in God's Word, and conversations became profound

In God's strength you blazed the trail ahead
"Stay close to God" you always said
Growing stronger and stronger as the cancer progressed
All things known and believed were put to the test

Through the fires and waters we at different times went
While God taught us only on Him to depend
Refuge was sought in the shelter of His wings
As we learned more and more that to Him we must cling

Faith and trust are hallmarks of your trial
As physical and spiritual testing occurred, while all the while
You helped me see that life from God was a gift
Something to be cherished, and not something merely lived

Your life on earth is ending earlier than we thought
But we know that your soul with Christ's blood has been bought
It's amazing the gift God will give, setting you free
Cancer to be banished from your body eternally

Now as you enter the end of your race
Through the trials and hardships you have been given God's grace
Because you love God, your crown will to you be bestowed
God's name has been glorified as you in His presence will soon go

"Because she loves Me I will rescue her," said her LORD
"She called and I answered by opening heaven's door
I have been with her always throughout all the strife
And now am about to honor her with long eternal life" (Psalm 91)

Love, your sister in Christ, Helena

Six

The Radiation

But those who hope in the LORD will renew their strength.
They will soar on wings like eagles; they will run and not grow weary,
they will walk and not be faint.

ISAIAH 40:31

Welcoming my younger sister to Australia a few short weeks after my brother and his wife had returned to Canada, was wonderful. I loved being with her, but, even more than that, I loved how well our children—who had never met her before—responded to her presence in our home. Perhaps it was because she looked so much like me and her mannerisms resembled mine that they felt like they had their mother back. She would make their lunches, meet them at the bus-stop after school, listen to their home readers, take them for walks, and do so many more things I had used to do, but now struggled to do. It was bittersweet to see.

Two weeks after her arrival, radiation began. It was to be something of a marathon—six weeks of Monday to Friday treatments. But even though radiation was doled out daily, instead of chemo's three weekly dose, it was still considered to be an easier treatment. I guess it's all relative. You're trading poisoning your body with chemicals to beaming radiation into it.

True, you don't lose your hair, but then again, I no longer had any hair left to lose!

The few weeks' break between chemo and radiation allowed me to regain some strength, and I felt quite strong as I embarked on this next phase. I was even well enough to start running again. The break also helped me consolidate spiritually. I was spending more time with God, and He was revealing Himself to me in intimate ways which I treasured greatly. I felt that through His power I could do immeasurably more than I could ever have imagined doing. If someone had said to me five years ago that I would have to endure operations, chemotherapy, and radiation, I would have said that I could never do it. And here, by the grace and strength of God, I was doing it.

Since radiation was Monday to Friday, I got the drill down pat rather quickly. It went something like this: My sister would drop the kids off at the bus stop and return to drive me to the radiation clinic. I would take my Bible, devotion book, and music with me. Upon arrival, I would swipe my card to register my attendance, go to my cubicle to change into my hospital gown (stored in my personal locker) and then go to the "patient only" waiting room. There were generally three or four others there, all waiting for their turn. When my name got called, I entered the room containing the radiation machine. Going into this room always gave me goose bumps, even though the staff were very friendly and would do all they could to put me at ease. I would ask them to connect my music to their speakers, which they gladly did. It really helped to have my Christian music playing softly while the staff set everything up. Both my body and the machine had to be meticulously positioned with the measurements absolutely precise. I couldn't so much as sneeze or the process would need to begin all over again!

When everything was ready, the technicians would turn the music louder (on my request!) and go into the control room. It was time for the buzzing noise to begin, while the arms of the radiation machine moved around me like a satellite in space, its rays taking aim at my body. I was on my own in the room, just me, the buzzing noise, and the laser show. I forced myself to focus on the lyrics of the music, to sort of leave my body lying on the table, and get my mind to contemplate on things above. This was very effective, and I would no longer feel alone in the room. Then, just as quickly as radiation began, it was over. The machine stopped buzzing, moving, and shooting and I could return to my cubicle, get dressed, put on my essential oils (I wasn't allowed to have them on during treatment) and return to the waiting room to rejoin my sister or whoever else had driven me in that day.

The music I played during radiation would often be Psalms from the Bible (my favorites being Psalm 23, Psalm 91, and Psalm 121) or other Christian music containing hope and promise. My fellow patients, waiting for their turn down the hall, could clearly hear my music and soon I was known as "the music lady."

Next, it was off to the hospital cafeteria and hope that they had opened their kitchen so we could have some hot fries with our coffees. Then, finally, it was time to return to life outside the radiation clinic until the next day, when the process would be repeated all over again.

Since, for the most part, I saw the same people every day in the patient-only waiting room, I got to know them quite well. There was one man who was having radiation for brain cancer. He would peck away at his laptop, while telling me how busy he was as a director on the board of some important company. They were in the middle of doing a merger or a takeover, something of great consequence, or so he seemed to think. He found it very frustrating that he couldn't type properly, due to his brain cancer. He treated his illness as a most unwelcome interruption to his very important life. He also found the treatment very hard to tolerate. Because of these reasons, he was considering stopping radiation. I empathized with him, somewhat, having had a friend who had just had radiation of the brain. She stopped, not because she had more important things to do, but because the treatment was just too taxing. So I said to the businessman: *"Well, if you are ready for what's on the other side when you die, then by all means, don't come back tomorrow for more."* The next day he was there in the waiting room. The laptop was nowhere in sight. I said: *"You're back!"* He just looked at me. Maybe he wasn't prepared for Who he would meet on the other side, the way my friend had been. I pray that before he dies, he will be.

Then there was the tough Harley biker that, at first, I was even scared to have eye contact with. But cancer is a great leveller. You can be a housewife, you can be the CEO of a big corporation, you can be a bikie, or you can be the Prime Minister for all cancer cares. You're all in the waiting room, all waiting to get buzzed by radiation, all waiting to see what the radiation will do, all waiting to see whether you will live or die. Waiting. It is something all cancer patients have to do, but never quite get used to doing. And because you waited together, you ended up becoming part of each other's lives, sometimes just for a season, sometimes longer. It presented opportunities to share the gospel with people who otherwise you may never have shared it with.

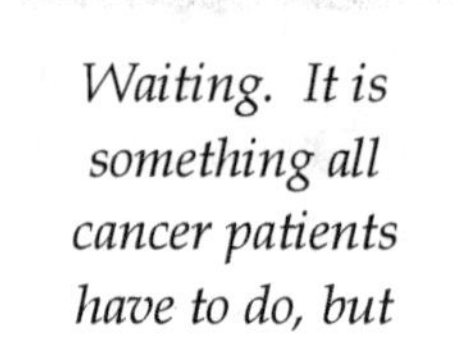

Waiting. It is something all cancer patients have to do, but never quite get used to doing.

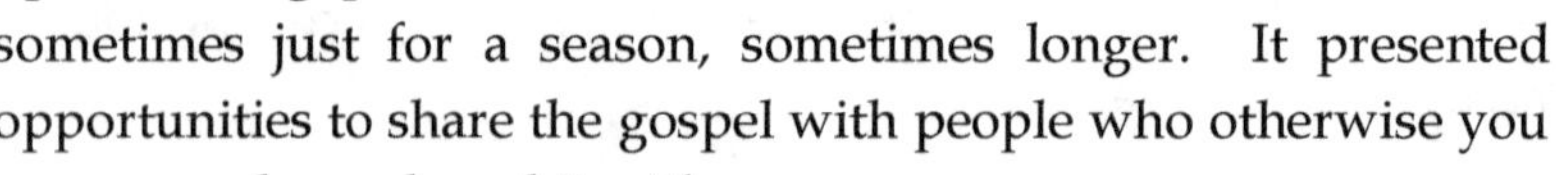

Over time, radiation proved to be quite demanding mentally. Going every single day, seeing other cancer patients every single day, and being reminded of the fight going on in your body every single day was quite draining. Often, after treatment, I would go to a place called "Solaris" for rejuvenation and time to process the events of my life. It was a special place run by beautiful volunteers whose sole aim was to provide love and support to those going through cancer. They gave complimentary massages, provided resources, but most importantly they were always ready with a hug and encouragement. Sometimes my sister and I would go there and just sit in their recliners and relax before going home. Solaris was a real gift to me during this time of treatment, providing a place of processing, a place of transition before returning to the normal world once again.

As the days turned into weeks, I began to feel more and more weary. The radiation, although not as hard on my body as chemo, made me very tired. I was so thankful that my sister was capably running the household. In the meantime, her husband had flown over from Canada to join her and also help out. I had such confidence in my sister that I no longer even bothered trying to do my bit, not that I had energy to do much anyways. I wondered how we would survive when she left with three weeks of radiation still to go, but I was almost too tired to worry about that either.

When my sister returned to Canada it was very difficult, not only for me, but also the children. They had really felt, in my sister, as if they had received their Mom back, only to lose her again.

Although she was no longer there to help out, the provisions didn't stop. It was amazing and humbling to see so many others step in and help out. My youngest brother and his wife by this time were also planning a trip Down Under to lend some assistance. I was greatly looking forward to seeing them and having them meet our children.

In the meantime, my husband decided to take two days off work per week to help with running the household until radiation was finished. Everyone seemed tired and some days things in the home started to wear pretty thin. We all needed a lot of patience and love.

As I neared the end of radiation treatment, I wrote this contemplative update to my closest family and friends:

> Radiation—six visits to go (twenty-two completed!) putting me pretty close to 80 percent. It was so nice that my husband took two days off this week to go with me and spoil me with a picnic at the beach today . . .
>
> I have been thinking a lot about this text in Hebrews 2:10:
>
> "In bringing many sons and daughters to glory, it was fitting that God, for whom and through whom everything exists,

> should make the pioneer of their salvation perfect through what He suffered."
>
> I'm starting to understand, or maybe appreciate more and more, that Jesus, the Head of the Church of which I am part of the body, knows to a much fuller extent than any of us will ever know, what it is like to suffer. This fills me with much comfort, realizing too that He intercedes now before the Father, telling Him about my suffering, understanding it so well, having lived life East of Eden Himself and walking the hard road so our road would never be as hard.
>
> And so I'm starting to realize that God is busy re-creating me, teaching me to find my security in Him and not in the circumstances or even people around me, as He continues His work of bringing me to glory.
>
> I pray that He will continue to walk beside me and be my strength and also give my husband and the children what they need.

My church family continued to be the hands and feet of Christ. After my sister left, they picked up the slack, sometimes meeting my needs before I even became aware of them, and greatly assisting my husband who was trying to hold everything together. Sometimes we thought we needed a social secretary just to keep track of who was driving me to treatment, who was doing the school runs, who was cooking the meals, and who was cleaning the house.

In somewhat of a blur, the days passed, one at a time. Everyone was fed and everything happened that needed to happen. Before long, the final day arrived. The 28/28 day. Yes, the last day of treatment was finally here. I awoke that morning to mixed feelings. All these people—both staff and other patients—had been my world for the last six weeks and now it was time to say goodbye. It was difficult to wean myself off the medical community that had become my second family. I was amazed at how God had brought certain people into my world for this certain season and how now it was time to let go. All of us were returning to our own futures, all of us were going back to our own lives and destinies, both temporal and eternal. All of us had been changed in one way or another.

Finishing radiation, I realized that physically I had done all I could—enduring treatments, eating healthy, and exercising. Spiritually, I had also done what I could—investing in my relationship with God, giving things over to Him, and trusting that He would turn them to my good. Now it was time to wait and to recover. Our family was tired and ready for a time of consolidation and rejuvenation. I saw evidence of exhaustion in everyone, expressed in their own unique ways.

On the evening of the 28/28 day, my husband spoke to our children before devotions to let them know that all the treatments had been completed. I felt like I was looking at them for the first time in weeks—*really* looking at them. He told them about how courageously I had fought the battle. I gazed intently at all six of our beautiful children, who just sat there, unmoving, unemotional, and unresponsive. Not happy, not sad. In fact, they seemed expressionless. Then it hit me. They were detached! Had they pulled back from me emotionally in case I didn't survive? I didn't know. I was too tired to ask, and they were too weary to answer.

While I could sympathize with the children's reaction and knew that they loved me in spite of their detachment, it still left me feeling somewhat upset. Did I go through so much for such ambivalence? I felt like I had returned home after a long battle to find I no longer had a relevant place in their lives. Did they still view me as their mother? Or was I just a cancer patient to them? I prayed for God to gather these, His lambs, in His arms and carry them close to His heart in this, their time of transition and confusion. I reminded myself that their ways and my way wasn't hidden from the LORD, and that He, in His time, would renew our strength.

I lay in bed that night feeling like I had been catapulted back into a world where I no longer knew how to function or feel. I had prayed so hard to stay on this earth with my family, but had also been readied to release this temporal existence. Where did I belong? I was confused and overwhelmed about transitioning back into normalcy, when I no longer knew what that even was.

I closed my eyes and dreamed of soaring on Eagle's wings and was comforted.

Seven

The Transition

Therefore, if anyone is in Christ, the new creation has come:
The old has gone, the new is here!

2 CORINTHIANS 5:17

The months following treatment were months of major adjustment. We had been plunged into a new normal and began to slowly realize that things could not and would not ever be the same again.

I could never again be someone who could live a relatively carefree day-to-day existence, with my biggest worry being what to cook for dinner. Every time my back was sore, every time I felt a lump somewhere, every time I was more tired than usual, would I wonder whether the cancer was back? Would the children hold their collective breaths every time I had to see the doctor for something?

Then there was the post-treatment plan. How much surveillance was necessary? What was the right balance between God's sovereignty and our responsibility (you would think we had this worked out by now!). Where to from here? We wanted to do God's will, but weren't sure exactly what that was. The questions and decisions continued. How long would this uncertainty go on—for the rest of my life? What did moving forward look like?

Transitioning to a new normal was a huge adjustment on so many different fronts. I felt I was looking at everyday life with different glasses on. Everything had changed for me, while it appeared to stay the same for most everyone else.

My new life was filled with new sensations. It was like getting off a roller-coaster ride you had been on for such a long time that being on the ride with all its ups and downs had started to feel normal. Now the ride was over and you had been told to get off. You had wanted it to stop, wanted to get off, but now that it had and you had, you needed to learn how to walk on solid ground once again. But the ground no longer felt solid. Everything felt strange—frighteningly strange, abnormally strange. Where did I begin? I had to learn to go forward one step at a time, on tottering limbs, navigating in a world I scarcely recognized, interacting with people who scarcely seemed to recognize me.

How do I react to other cancer patients I came across in the grocery store, patients who were obviously in the middle of their treatments? I had never seen them before but now I saw them everywhere. How do I quieten the pendulum swing of feelings that continued to sweep over me? There were moments where I would mourn my losses until I thought my heart would break, and others where I felt incredible joy and thankfulness just to be alive.

How do I get ready for the days that left me so exhausted—mentally, emotionally, physically, and spiritually—that I even wondered if I had prayed for the wrong outcome? How do I handle the myriad of questions people had for me, how do I manage re-entering my children's lives in a tangible and meaningful way? How do I deal with people talking about ordinary things like the weather? Perhaps the one that required the most patience and wisdom was: how do I ever cope with people complaining about things that seemed so trivial and ridiculous to me?

My prayers became pleas for God to help me see that the goal of my life was to glorify Him through all my circumstances and exchanges and not to question Him through them all. I prayed that He would show me His way forward in my newly created life, that He would teach me how to live in this new normal, how to live the remainder of my days this side of heaven, giving Him the glory and showing love to my neighbor.

My prayers became pleas for God to help me see that the goal of my life was to glorify Him through all my circumstances and not to question Him through them all.

Who would've guessed this transition would be so heart-wrenching, so very difficult, and leave me feeling so restless? It didn't make sense. No one told me things would be like this—that I would feel like this.

As the weeks following radiation turned into months, I began to notice that my husband and children, and even our parents, started to slowly unthaw. It was almost like they dared to breathe once again—dream once again. Questions slowly emerged and emotions that were too raw earlier were shared. Everyone was busy processing. It was good for them. But I worried that if everyone else got to return to their old normal, would it just be me left behind? Would I be all alone?

I felt like a stranger in a strange land. I knew Christians were meant to feel like wayfaring strangers, like desert wanderers, but now I really felt like one and it felt strange! It was as C.S. Lewis once wrote: "If I find in myself a desire which no experience in this world can satisfy, the most probable explanation is that I was made for another world."[12] Was it possible that my feelings were now anchored by an increased awareness of my temporal existence?

---

[12] Lewis, *Mere Christianity*, 136–137.

I sensed Satan crouching at my door, waiting for me to falter, wanting me to have an ungrateful heart for everything God had done for me. I vacillated between two extremes—from holding on to life and living it with all I had, to giving up on ever feeling at home in this world again. I read in Hebrews that I was receiving a kingdom that could not be shaken (Hebrews 12:28), but when I embraced thoughts of this glorious kingdom, I in turn felt detached from the kingdom below. This left me feeling that I belonged nowhere. I had a thirst for perfection in a world that was broken, and these two things seemed at odds. I silently and inwardly groaned, longing to be clothed with my heavenly body.

I turned to my Bible time and time again and prayed for peace as I transitioned back into everyday life. I read the words of Psalm 46 to "be still" over and over again. I heard them resonate in the words of Paul to the Corinthians, directing them, and me, to live by faith and not by sight (2 Corinthians 5:7).

It was hard enough finding peace with the changes to my body, but it was much harder to claim this peace for my soul. It wasn't that things weren't well with my soul, but more that things were different, and I had to get used to this different. I now possessed a heightened awareness that life on this earth was transient. I had lost my feeling of belonging, of attachment. I had gained the knowledge that I would never truly belong, until the day of complete restoration. God had brought me through this desert march, not to starve me, but to change me, to re-create me. And He had. And He would continue to. I had to trust Him with these changes as I moved forward.

God wasn't finished teaching me, re-creating me, refining me. I couldn't say I had arrived, because quite simply I hadn't. The best was yet to come, but wasn't here yet. I knew that now. The arrival, the closing of the circle, would need to wait until the final day, the day when my re-creation would be totally complete, where my image would mirror that of my Savior's, where I would glorify God in perfection and eternity.

And so, as I transitioned back into a world I struggled to recognize, I thanked God that He was busy with me, preparing me in this life for the life to come, gifting me His Spirit as a guarantee of what would one day come: perfection of body and soul. As time progressed, I became more comfortable with my new life, living a day at a time, while enjoying and giving thanks for little moments along the way.

I was being released. There was no longer any medical staff to hover over me and make sure I was well. But that was fine. Because there was One who was—the One who was fashioning me, compelling me through Christ's love to live for Him. The old had gone and the new was here. It was time to embrace it.

Maybe this new normal wouldn't be so bad after all.

To our family, *August 17, 2016*

I had my post radiation follow up CT scan last week; on the same day they organized for an ultrasound with a core needle biopsy to investigate a suspicious mass that had only been discovered a week or so prior (it was scary finding that!). You may wonder why you didn't know about this. It's because we are trying not to take everyone with us on the roller-coaster called cancer. Because we need to get used to living the life of testing at least for the next few years and we want life to be as normal as it can be during that time. Having said that, I sure did miss your prayers as how could you pray about something you didn't know about!

Once again, waiting for the results was not easy. We know we are not to be anxious about tomorrow, and to give thanks in everything. We know God's promises are true and that we need to focus on God and not our circumstances. We know that we need to give things over to the God who made us, the God who loves us, and the God who saves us. This is a lesson we find we need to learn over and over again, and so the wait was not always easy. I especially had to try really hard not to think about whether I had to go through chemo again. To not make decisions before I had to make them.

We are humbled, therefore, that in spite of our struggles with total trust in God's plan for our lives, He has answered our prayers. Yesterday we found out that not only was the CT scan showing clear, the biopsy came back as benign (no cancer). Praise the LORD!!!!!!

We felt like a load had been lifted off our shoulders. Helena felt like doing cartwheels down the hospital corridor! Instead, we hopped on our bikes and went for a cycle in the sunshine through King's Park followed by a lunch at the cutest Bistro in Perth complete with a Pina Colada (it was the best!).

Being under a surveillance program means that Helena will have further tests, most likely every half a year or so. But we will continue to pray for the Holy Spirit to work trust in our hearts, trust that God is writing the story of our and our children's lives and that this story is for our good and His glory. And so we go forward in His grace, enjoying each day as a gift from His Fatherly hand.

PART TWO:

THE PROVISIONS

Every good and perfect gift is from above.

JAMES 1:17

When God led Israel out of Egypt into the desert, en route to the Promised Land, He gave them wide-ranging provisions for their journey. Their shoes didn't wear out, they were provided with manna and quails for food, and water from the rock. In addition to these physical provisions, God comforted, strengthened, and protected them by visually showing His presence in the form of a cloud by day and fire by night. They were never alone in their refining journey to become God's holy people, and they received many good and perfect gifts from God that enabled them to arrive at their destination.

We, too, as God's children, are never alone in our refining. We, too, need to believe that God will give us exactly what we need for both body and soul along the way. Many of us have been taught about these provisions from our youth. Our parents, our pastors, our teachers, and the Bible itself are all means that God uses to assure us that He will never leave or forsake us and will fulfill all our needs in Christ as we journey from the temporal to the eternal.

Theologically, we know all this—it's all part of what we have believed since childhood. We have been encouraged to trust in God's promises no matter what happens, but now cancer was happening and these promises needed to be appropriated in a way they never quite had before. My theology needed to take a dramatic leap into my day-to-day circumstances, and it was a leap that was bigger than I thought it would be. It was an exciting leap, but it also felt a bit overwhelming and even somewhat frightening.

My theology needed to take a dramatic leap into my day-to-day circumstances, and it was a leap that was bigger than I thought it would be.

Maybe you think that it would be easier to keep a bit of distance between you and God—that distance you perhaps always had but didn't realize and unknowingly had become comfortable with. Maybe you're feeling a bit like the Israelites at the foot of Mount Sinai when they said something like this to Moses: Can't you just go and talk to God? This is all a little much for us (Exodus 20:19).

Every journey requires preparation. You're about to embark on a journey that will not leave you unchanged; a journey that will not only impact you physically, but also relationally, mentally, emotionally and, most consequentially, spiritually. This will be no short trip around the block. Desert journeys are long and arduous and are not without danger. You're going to need provisions. God has them readily available.

You will be thirsty and there will be times you cannot walk another step without the Living Water God provides. The more you drink, the stronger you will feel Christ's Spirit equipping and sustaining you, strengthening you. At times you will even be so strong that you will support others who are struggling with seeing you suffer, rather than being supported by them.

So many Bible stories exemplify this concept of God's provisions. Just think of the Apostle Paul. He had a thorn in his flesh to keep him from becoming conceited. But God provided grace that was sufficient for Paul, power that was made perfect in Paul's weakness. That led Paul to proclaiming that he boasts in his weakness, so that Christ's power may rest on him (2 Corinthians 12:9). We, too, can be assured that God will withhold no good thing from those who love Him. He didn't withhold what was needed for Paul, He didn't withhold what was needed for Israel, and He won't withhold it from us when we ask. Then we can consider it pure joy when we face our trials, because we know it will produce perseverance and that this perseverance will cause us to become mature and complete (James 1:2–4).

Considering suffering as pure joy does not negate the harshness that suffering's journey brings. I will not minimize it, because it is something that must be endured, and enduring it can be extremely difficult and fraught with danger. On the other hand, I want us to lift our eyes and see the beautiful provisions God gives along the way, provisions made possible through our Savior. Christ suffered so that we can have a restored relationship with our Father, a Father who delights to give us provisions.

These gifts can't ever be separated from our need for them. How would we know how wonderful it is to receive help unless we had need of help? You may wish you were well and not in need of these special provisions. But think about it this way: if we didn't need help, would we need God? Charles Spurgeon once wrote: "We have great demands, but Christ has great supplies. Between here and Heaven we shall have, perhaps, greater wants than we have yet known; but, all along, every halting place is ready, provender is laid up, good cheer is stored, nothing has been overlooked. The commissariat of the Eternal is absolutely perfect."[13]

It is somewhat complicated to divide provisions into different categories, because many, if not all, overlap. This book does so in order to allow the reader to go straight to a relevant section they may identify with or need extra encouragement in, whether it be relationally, mentally, emotionally, physically, or spiritually. The

---

[13] Spurgeon, "He shall be Great," Metropolitan Tabernacle Pulpit, Volume 30.

spiritual provision is unique in that it provides an overarching umbrella for all the other provisions. One thing to keep in mind while reading this section is that everyone is different, and God's provisions to one may look different than His provisions to another. He knows all of His children and what is best for them.

But the greatest provision during your refining is sure to be God's presence. Did you know that when gold is being refined, the refiner stays right beside the object of refining, constantly checking whether the temperature has to go up or come down? Constantly checking on whether the process is achieving the desired result? The refiner never leaves the side of what's being refined. The same is true of God. He is right beside you. It's as Isaiah writes: "When you pass through the waters, I will be with you . . . when you walk through the fire, you will not be burned" (Isaiah 43:2). Indeed, "Never will I leave you; never will I forsake you" (Hebrews 13:5).

I didn't need to do my desert trek alone, and neither do you. My Refiner was by my side, giving me all I needed to make it through—through my temporal existence or through to my eternal home. Cancer is not a win or lose situation; my battle wasn't a battle that I had to win. The battle that did need to be won has been won by Christ, when He died and was raised from the dead, conquering death and Satan for all time, conquering death so all those who believe in Him can live. I was a winner already!

It would be naive to think that provisions aren't sometimes misused or mishandled. We live in a fallen world, and when fallen creatures are used to bestow God's provisions, sin can rear its head, causing pain. That's why it is important to examine situations and reactions when receiving God's perfect provisions through imperfect instruments. We must be aware that the devil wants us to stumble over provisions rather than be strengthened by them.

Let's also be careful not to repeat the rebellion of Israel on their desert march. Instead of being thankful for what they received, they were unthankful. They grumbled and tested God continually, making demands of Him through Moses (Numbers 11:13). In spite of this, God, in His grace, still gave His people not only the food they needed, but the meat they wanted. He gave them more provisions than were required to make the journey. And He does the same for me and for you. In His great mercy God gives good gifts to His children.

However, never mistake provisions for permission to cease travelling. C.S. Lewis, in his book *The Problem of Pain* makes this important point: "Our Father refreshes us on the journey with some pleasant inns, but will not encourage us to mistake them for home."[14] We receive provisions, and must use them to walk on.

So, walk on, dear pilgrim, with an open hand, and accept with thanksgiving the good and perfect gifts of provision which come down from your Father—the Father of the heavenly lights.

---

[14] Lewis, *The Problem of Pain,* 116.

Eight

The Relational Provision

Love must be sincere.

ROMANS 12:9

"Expect the unexpected." That's the good advice my cousin gave when it came to receiving support from other people. In hindsight, it was advice we did well to take to heart, but, even still, we were nowhere near ready to appreciate or navigate the relational provisions provided to us. The wisdom of the Bible and life experience had both been teachers in the highs and lows of interpersonal relationships, but cancer put relationships into an entirely new light.

God will extend His love to you through many others as you walk the road of cancer. This is a most beautiful and encouraging provision, and the vast majority of these interactions will be an incredible source of help to you. But, it won't all be smooth sailing. In fact, you will discover some unexpected difficulties, and will need to learn to deal with them as the Spirit enables and the Word instructs—with love.

One relational challenge that soon presented itself was letting those near and dear to us know where things were at in the ever-changing landscape of my diagnosis. The prayers and support from our family and friends were a beautiful provision of God's love and care, but keeping everyone informed was laborious and time-consuming and, soon, overwhelming. Providing information and updates by email proved the best course of handling outward communication. Writing these also gave us the much-needed opportunity to process what was happening in our lives. This proved very beneficial, especially since it required a verbalizing of truths that existed but often felt surreal.

Receiving Christ's love as expressed through relationships with others was gratefully appreciated; especially when people let us know they were praying for us and included some sort of scriptural encouragement in their dialogue. Email and cards were a great way to receive support. Visits and phone calls have their strengths, but the advantage of email and cards proved to be that we could read them when we felt able to; they would simply be there waiting for us, but not demanding our immediate attention when we didn't feel up to it.

Because of the fall into sin, when God uses people to convey His love and care to you, they will sometimes fail. They will sometimes say or do the wrong thing.

You may have relational expectations. Something that's important to remember as you deal with varied reactions to your cancer diagnosis is this: people aren't God. This seems obvious, but, unfortunately, we often expect people to do the perfect thing and say the perfect thing. Going through cancer gives you heightened contact with many different types of people, at a level you may not have experienced before. It's of great help to stop and realize that God's direct provisions in His relationship with you are always perfect: the Bible will never disappoint, the Spirit will always comfort, and you will always feel understood by God.

However, because of the fall into sin, when God uses people to convey His love and care to you, they will sometimes fail. Even the most reliable friend is bound to make mistakes along the way, sometimes lapsing, sometimes saying or doing the wrong thing. And what makes this doubly challenging is that you are more sensitive to these failings than you might usually be. Many times you will feel disappointed by others and you must ensure that it doesn't grow into resentment or bitterness. Nevertheless, in spite of these failings, relationships with people are still a most valuable provision of the love and care God extends to you. Always remember that love, when sincere, covers a multitude of sins (1 Peter 4:8).

Something that warrants contemplation is the setting of expectations for how people react to your situation. You are sure to be surprised by some of their responses. Generally, you will find four contingents of people:

1. Those you expect to be there for you, and they are;
2. Those you don't expect to be there for you, and they aren't;
3. Those you don't expect to be there for you, and they are;
4. Those you expect to be there for you, and they aren't.

It's this last group that can cause you the most grief and sorrow if you aren't forewarned and prepared to interact with them in a Christian manner.

When you are first diagnosed with cancer, you think about the impact it will have on you personally. After all, you're the one with the diagnosis, right? And make no mistake—you will be greatly impacted. But it soon becomes clear that your cancer journey is part of a much bigger picture. You will find it humbling to see God at work in ways and in people you would never dream of or expect. Remember that God is at work in everyone's life that is touched by your cancer, not just at work in you. This is because Christ is the Head of the Church, a Church where members are not independent of one other, but, rather, dependant on each other; a Church that is growing together under the Headship of Christ. We'll explore this in greater detail in *The Weaving* (chapter 16).

Before we develop the relational provision any further, I want to share with you something that was shared with me and my husband shortly after my diagnosis, which we found very useful. It's called "comfort in, dump out" and is based on the "Ring Theory"[15] of concentric circles. It goes something like this:

THE RING THEORY
Draw a circle and put the cancer patient's name inside;
Draw a larger circle around the first one and write the name of the person next closest to the crisis, such as a husband;
In each larger ring place the next closest grouping of persons. This could be children, then parents, next relatives, followed by close friends, church community, work colleagues, and finishing with acquaintances.

The governing principal is that the person with the immediate crisis gets to express their emotions and feelings to anyone outside of their circle. They are in the center circle, in their own little ring. The person in the next circle, say the husband, also needs someone to express his feelings and worries to, but he can't "dump" on the person in the center because he needs to support that person. He can only extend outward. The Ring Theory ensures that you are being helpful to those in rings smaller than you, that you are supporting them, and not having them support you—"comfort in, dump out."

This system may have its imperfections, but, generally, it is a good rule of thumb in helping people to decide whether to just listen to their friend who has been diagnosed or whether to assault her

[15] Silk and Goldman, "Ring Theory."

with all their own worries and concerns about how her diagnosis is going to impact them. Otherwise, you will find you end up becoming the provider of support, instead of the receiver of it.

We're now ready to break our relational provisions down into a few distinct categories and uncover both the blessings and challenges of each associated group.

Your Spouse

This isn't only your journey. What you're going through will have an immeasurable impact on your spouse. When he vowed on your wedding day to be with you "in sickness and in health" he had no idea what those words could, one day, entail.

Now he does.

His load is heavy. Not only is he the sole parent much of the time, he has to keep the house running somewhat normally while still trying to go to his regular nine to five job as often as he can and function in that capacity. In addition, he must fulfill these multiple tasks while at the same time protecting and being there for you, fulfilling your needs as best he can. This is a huge ask. As time passes, he gets weary.

Support

Spouses can be inadvertently overlooked in prayer and support, when sometimes they can need it even more than the person enduring the suffering. They may not think they need it, they may say they don't need it, and some will certainly need more encouragement than others. But the fact is, you are your spouse's best friend, but you are putting all your energy into putting one foot in front of the other, and so, can't really fulfill that role for him.

At times this made me feel guilty, and maybe that's why I often longed for someone to step in and simply be there for my husband in a quiet, strong way. How I prayed that godly men would push past their hesitancy and reach out to him.

Men are fixers, at least my husband is, and my cancer was something that he couldn't fix. It left him with empty hands which led him on his own refinement journey. He also needed to be able to process and talk about his feelings. My heart ached at times as I saw him walking this road, and I would have given anything for him to have had more love and care extended to him.

Attacks

Over time, you both begin to feel run-down. You're weary, he's weary, and often you're called to make major decisions on a few hours' sleep while trying to run a busy household and making frequent road trips to the hospital. It was a challenging time for us.

Reading the Bible and praying together provided a strong buffer against attacks on our marriage during this intense time. However, there were situations where we felt differently about things, and even though we loved each other deeply, we couldn't always protect our feelings from being hurt. We were just too vulnerable and tired, and there were times we didn't understand why the other felt or reasoned the way they did. If you're not careful, this is where fracture lines can begin to appear in the foundation of a perfectly good marriage.

If you're not careful, this is where fracture lines can begin to appear.

For us, there was one specific instance when our marriage struggled. I am sharing this with you to prepare you, because I wasn't expecting it—which made it so much harder to deal with. I am sharing this with you to show you how important it is to overcome disappointment on your journey and instead let perceived failings drive you to total dependence on God, not total dependence on your spouse. This was a crucial and painful lesson I had to learn.

The attack happened while we were busy weighing up treatment options, discussing what our responsibility was in light of God's sovereignty. We saw things differently, and my spouse ended this particular conversation with somewhat doubting my trust in God while I queried what I thought was his lack of responsibility in the dire situation we were in. It hurt me that my best friend, the one constantly at my side, could question what was of paramount importance to me: my trust in God! It cut, and it cut deeply. Attacks such as this needed to be combatted by realizing that the blessing of a loving spouse is arguably the top relational provision you have, second only to God's presence Himself.

Blessing of a Loving Spouse

Instead of dwelling on the disappointing times, rather dwell on all the other times—and there will be many, many more—where he stood by your side through thick and thin, supporting you, loving you, understanding you. When seen through this lens, and realizing none of us is 100 percent perfect, not your spouse, not you, it will become easier to let go of the disappointments. It encourages you to overlook perceived offenses, and, instead, acknowledge what a rich provision your marriage actually is.

My husband amazed me with the strength, integrity, and love he showed throughout my time of cancer. I'm overwhelmed when I bring to mind all the loving acts of service—the cups of tea he made, all the hours of driving to appointments and surgeries, waiting with me in countless waiting rooms, sleeping in the car during long surgeries, washing my hair when I couldn't shower, running my medication charts with precision, and countless other servant hood tasks. He did all these things while running the household and being a father to our children, and somehow managing to still go to work and provide an income. Pause and consider what a wonderful blessing your spouse is. Focus on the 95 percent right he does, and not the 5 percent he possibly got wrong.

Lessons Learned

It took some time and a lot of prayer before I realized that I was making a big mistake. I was looking to my husband to be my perfect savior and deliverer, putting him in the place where there was only room for one Savior and Deliverer.

When, oh when, would I learn that my dependence had to rest in God? When, oh when, would I look to God first, before anyone else? At the end of the day, it is all about God's relationship with me, and mine with Him. All other relationships are gifts, but fallen gifts, imperfect gifts. Why was I expecting perfection from a fellow fallen soul? Why was I expecting perfection from my husband when I was so far from perfect myself? I should be rejoicing that this was the one and only time he disappointed me when the journey was so perilously hard. I should be thankful for the provision God gave me through him. I should be mindful that this was hard for him too.

God was teaching me a valuable lesson: to beware of the enemy. And, no, the enemy most certainly wasn't my husband. It was none other than Satan—Satan, who loves turning testing into temptations. Satan, telling me lies, telling me that if my husband really loved me he would never have questioned my trust in God. Satan, telling me it wasn't possible that there were different ways of seeing this, but that my way was the best way forward. The deceiver, as always, was up to his old tricks of wrapping deadly deceit in a modicum of truth.

Provisions and pitfalls, testing and temptation, truth and lies. They were all there, right in front of me. I prayed for the Holy Spirit to help me navigate the right path—the path of light over the path of darkness. I prayed that the Holy Spirit would help me to realize my greatest need was fulfilled by my Father in heaven. To realize if I had to let everything go, to open up my fingers and release everything or everyone else in total surrender, that, in His strength, I could.

A husband's perspective . . .

I didn't realize it at the time. But it crystallized later, much later, when the journey was over, when someone asked me in the church parking lot how it had been for me.

As I grappled with putting my emotions into words, it came:

Helena often felt the need for comfort. For shelter. For a hiding place. To be carried. She found that with God. He gathered her, as a hen gathers its chicks under her feathers. A warm, cosy, safe place. As an eagle carries its young.

But for me, it was not so. I needed to be strong. A warrior. Standing, fierce. Facing the onslaught. And I found that too. With God. He was my Rock – that's what He was. My unshakeable, secure foothold where I could stand and not feel shifting ground. Where I could firmly place my feet as a warrior needs to do when he's engaging in battle. That was how I felt. I found it in the Psalms – David, the warrior King, firmly standing, finding his strength.

Helena thought I needed support. What she didn't realize was that having God and her was all I needed. It was hard going at times. I found it difficult when people seemed to ignore the "elephant in the room." I found it frustrating that I couldn't "fix it." I found it challenging that we had little energy left for one another.

But, throughout it all, I knew that God would not fail. He was my Rock. And when all was said and done, He was what I needed the most.

I was reminded of a quote from Corrie ten Boom that my cousin Caroline had once emailed me, a quote I thought about often, a powerful quote borne from a woman's enduring horrendous conditions in a concentration camp. She wrote: "You can never learn that Christ is all you need, until Christ is all you have."[16]

I needed my husband. But I needed Christ more. I couldn't take my husband with me into the operating theatre. But Christ would be there. My husband couldn't be a perfect relational provision for me, but Jesus was. Only Jesus Christ is capable of perfectly fulfilling every need I have. I was learning not to expect others to take His rightful place in my life.

Charles Spurgeon would say that God was training me on the "highlands of affliction"[17] to be a good soldier. What He was teaching would stand me in good stead for receiving His relational provisions with love, in spite of their weaknesses; teaching me that I wasn't exactly perfect, either, and that there had been many times where I had been the flawed provision.

Your Children

Depending on their ages and characters, your children may be a provision to you or you may be a provision to them, or most likely it will be a combination of the two.

As a Mom, your children and their spiritual growth are among your top priorities. So many times I would pray to God that this journey we were on as a family would strengthen—and not weaken—their faith.

I was so thankful that my children were God's children. He had made promises to each one of them at their baptisms, promises to be their covenant God and turn whatever happened in their lives to their good. I often reminded God of these promises.

---

[16] ten Boom, "Corrie ten Boom Quotes."

[17] Spurgeon, "Terrible Convictions and Gentle Drawings," Sermon 313.

What They Learned

Our children learned so much as they lived the day-to-day of having a mother with cancer. They learned about the power of prayer and the ways God answers prayer—with a *yes, no,* or *wait.* They also learned about the fallen state of the world, the transitory nature of life, and they sought clarity about the life to come. These days contained many teachable moments for our children, teaching birthed in pain, but teaching that they would never forget. God was busy inscribing their hearts.

No one expects these covenant saplings to have to navigate their way through grown-up storms, but in the end, that was God's call to make and not mine. I wasn't in charge. And He decreed this to be part of their upbringing. I had to trust that God would take care of our children through this journey in the same way He was taking care of me. But, as a parent, I found it much easier to trust God with what He was doing in my life than with what He was doing in the lives of my children.

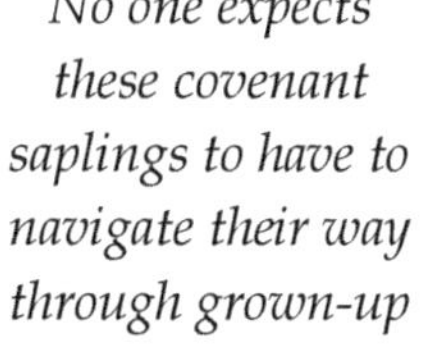

No one expects these covenant saplings to have to navigate their way through grown-up storms, but in the end, that was God's call to make and not mine.

I had to let go. I had to be willing to climb Mount Moriah and sacrifice my children to God's greater purposes, even though I sometimes questioned the means God was using to accomplish these purposes. At times, this was extremely difficult, especially when witnessing their reactions toward God for what they perceived as unanswered prayer. They would try to eradicate their pain by cutting off Who they perceived was the source of their pain. Not only would they sometimes push God away, they would occasionally even push me away for the very same reason.

But what they didn't realize, and what I tried to teach them, was that by seeking to rid the pain from their hearts, they were at the very same time cutting off their source of comfort in the midst of this pain. I tried to explain that as covenant children, they had been born into and were being raised under the umbrella of God's love, a love that would not let them go. They were safe! And so, they had to learn to trust in God's plan, just as we all did.

What They Needed

How I prayed for my children! How it hurt me to see their hurt. How I wanted to just kiss their aching hearts and make things better. But I couldn't. Many times I longed to have more opportunities and more energy to help them navigate their way through this quagmire. I was so appreciative of friends who realized the quandary I was in, and would step up and offer their love and care to our children on my behalf. This was immeasurably comforting to me.

Our children's need for support became really obvious one evening when we were sitting around the dinner table. As we had done pretty much from the beginning of the cancer journey, I would read out the cards that had arrived in the post that day. After one such reading session of five or so cards, one of the children unleashed what I'm sure was something that was waiting to be unleashed by all of his siblings: "It's all about you, isn't it, Mom! Your cancer, what you're going through. You get all the prayers, all the attention, but what about us?" The penny dropped. Our children needed people to be there for them too, people to encourage them. Their stability was under threat and they found this immeasurably difficult.

I encourage you, dear reader, if you know of a family where there is suffering, reach out to the children. They need it, and you will be answering many of the parents' prayers through your acts of kindness toward their children.

What They Gave

But it wasn't all hard. There was also beauty to be found in the children's brokenness: Beauty in seeing them on their knees, praying to God. Beauty in their after-school stories, telling me that their teachers reached out to them to see how they were doing, offered them assignment extensions when needed, and prayed for them and our family in class. The teachers were the people who saw our precious ones five days a week, the people on the coalface of our children's lives, and they rose to the challenge. I thanked God for them often.

Beauty was found in many little things too, like seeing the children standing in the garage waiting for me to come home after yet another operation or another treatment, with their beautiful, but anxious, faces. Beauty could be seen in their hugging me carefully so as not to hurt me, wanting to be near me but not wanting to be too much for me. Beauty, in going to my bedroom and finding cups of tea with little homemade cards waiting or finding Bible verses taped to my wall. These were some of the beautiful indications that God was sustaining them, comforting them, growing them, and giving them peace in the midst of their brokenness.

What We Explained

Communicating what cancer was to our children in a way that accounted for their different ages and characters was quite challenging, and took considerable thought. For my three younger boys, I used the example of having "bad LEGO® bricks" in my body that the doctor had to remove. Later, I described chemotherapy to them as destroying any remaining nasty LEGO bricks that my doctor couldn't see.

My eldest son needed reassurance that only some cases of breast cancer were terminal. Being a cricket fan, he found himself thinking about Glenn McGrath's wife, Jane, who died from breast cancer, wondering if that would happen to his Mom, as well.

My eldest daughter, who is interested in medicine, wanted to know specific details concerning my diagnosis, while my other daughter wasn't interested in technicalities, but desperately needed reassurance that her world as she knew it would not change.

Shielding our children from the truth was not helpful, but neither was inundating them with scenarios that might never occur. We always tried to be as honest as we could with them, using as much emotional intelligence as we could muster. It was crucial to elucidate to our children that God was at work in all our lives. That, because we live in a broken world, things like cancer happened, but things never happened outside God's control.

We underlined for our children time and again the promise contained in Romans 8—that in all things God works for the good of those who love Him. It even began to become a family refrain: "Romans 8 is great!" And the message of Romans 8 truly is great.

Shielding our children from the truth was not helpful, but neither was inundating them with scenarios that might never occur.

Maybe that's why one particular Mother's Day present I received the year of my diagnosis will be something I will always treasure. My preteen son came to me with a homemade gift. This was the same child who had been my prayer warrior; that is, until my cancer returned, after which he became convinced that prayer no longer worked. This son had been struggling. But this struggling only made his gift more priceless. He had been secretly busy in our neighbor's workshop for the past few weeks trying to complete it on time. As I unwrapped his present, my tears flowed freely. With a router, he had etched on wood in freeform writing the words of Romans 8:28, had painted the background, and had made a frame for it. Its message was ready to hang on our wall. Its message had already been engraved on our hearts.

A subject we also spoke to our children about was how God uses difficulties in our lives to grow us as Christians. We explained it in terms of pruning a tree. Living in the country, we had fruit trees all around us. Pruning was used to shape a tree and encouraged it to bear fruit. They had seen this firsthand when their Dad worked in the orchard. As parents, we explained, we too sometimes prune our children because we love them and want them to grow up to be a tree that will flourish. At times they might question Mom and Dad's love, because pruning often hurts. Well, we said, God also prunes and shapes those He loves so that they more and more resemble Jesus. He was busy shaping and refining our family right now. I'll never forget the words of my second youngest as he responded in the natural and unencumbered way children often do: "But *can't* God refine another family now?"

How They Coped

Children are all unique and will react and process things in different ways, at different times, using different means. Some will be verbal about their feelings, some will withdraw. Some will process, some will put their feelings into storage. Some will confront situations head on, while others will go and live in the land of denial. Similarly, all of my children responded and handled my cancer in their own distinct ways.

My oldest son ebbed and flowed with his reactions and emotions. Fear, denial, avoidance, and anger all played a part and by the time my second diagnosis occurred, he seemed done with it all. His coping mechanism was pushing it away. He just didn't want to know about it, and certainly didn't want to deal with it. He just couldn't do it anymore. He couldn't carry the burden, and didn't quite know how to lay the burden down. Seeing me without hair, as a result of my chemotherapy treatment, shattered him. It meant he could no longer deny what was so obviously happening.

My oldest daughter spent much of her free time on her beloved piano, playing vehemently during times of intense struggle. This was an effective way for her to release her emotions, and, as a result, she penned some beautiful and poignant songs. She also wrote in her diary, which helped her to process thoughts, especially when she felt overwhelmed. My daughter was quite emotionally adjusted. Something beautiful she did for me one day was to make a "book of envelopes." The instructions directed me to open an envelope whenever I needed some encouragement.

The envelope would have a picture or a short description on the outside that hinted at its contents. Inside, I would find a beautifully illustrated Bible verse or inspirational quote. I treasure this envelope book and have since also shared it with others suffering from cancer. It has proven to be a beautiful blessing.

My youngest daughter coped by keeping busy: cleaning the house, doing the laundry, and trying to behave perfectly. She put very high expectations on herself, as if by her doing everything right, everything would be all right. As a result, she would be hard on herself when she didn't get things done, or when she misbehaved. She would interpret this as failing me and letting me down. Her love tank needed constant refilling. She wore her heart on her sleeve and it was bittersweet to see her genuine love and concern for me.

My pre-teen son, the one who made me the Romans 8:28 engraving, began as my ardent prayer warrior, but then struggled to understand why God would heal me only for the cancer to return. This resulted in anger and doubt toward God and also toward me, wanting to cut off his perceived sources of pain. After my second diagnosis, he went from being a prayer warrior to being a prayer abstainer. He didn't want to pray. He didn't want to read his Bible. He didn't want me. His wound was raw. This was agonizing to watch, and I pleaded with God on many occasions that this son's pain would not damage his faith, but rather refine him, along with his other brothers and sisters. I prayed that this pain would mold and shape them all into godly men and women for the Kingdom. Over time, this became my most important and urgent prayer—even more important and urgent than my prayer for physical healing.

My eight-year-old son was much more factual and practical about matters. The LEGO explanation made a lot of sense to him. As long as his Mom appeared to be coping, he could handle things. His prayers were constant and unwavering, and I think his trust was much the same. As long as I didn't fall apart, he didn't fall apart.

My youngest son was five and met every day with exuberance. He is the sort of boy who throws open the door after getting out of bed and shouts: "Good morning, world!" My beautiful provision from the LORD, the child whom I discovered was in my womb on the morning of my fortieth birthday, was now, five years later, a source of constant sunshine in my life. By simply being there he reminded me of everything that was beautiful. His love, hugs, kisses, and enthusiasm comforted my soul in rich ways. At times it felt like he was going to and from God's throne room with buckets filled with God's love.

How They Changed

Watching your children suffer and relinquishing them into God's hands is not an easy process. But it is an important process, one that grows and matures them in their relationship with God, while at the same time cultivating their bonds with each other. This will be of lifelong, if not eternal, benefit.

I was so incredibly thankful to God for the provision of my children, even though seeing their pain brought me pain. The beauty was there, amidst the suffering. The beauty was there in the midst of the broken.

Your Parents

Having godly parents and parents-in-law is an indescribable gift and having them support me and my family through cancer, an immeasurable provision of God's grace. I know it was a hard time for them in so many ways. But they rarely, if ever, let me see how hard, always trying to be strong for me, reminding me of God's promises and praying those promises over me.

For my parents it was particularly difficult as they lived in Canada and I lived in Australia. Because they were in their early eighties, they were unable to make the trip over. This made them feel so helpless. The distance between us was more palpable than ever. All they could do was pray, which was actually the most powerful contribution they could have made anyways.

A daughter's diary entry . . .

Well, I learnt what it truly meant to trust in God again. On Wednesday Mum told me she had a bad infection that came in during her surgery for breast cancer. She said she had surgery scheduled but if she didn't feel better soon they'd move it up from a couple of months away to the next few days.

Before I left Thursday morning I peeked in and she told me she was feeling better, but when I came home on Friday night after having been away I was told she had surgery earlier on that day.

That's when all the memories came rushing back again: The feelings of protection, wanting to keep Mum happy and make her feel better by cleaning the house or playing nurse. The feelings of insecurity, having thousands of questions but feeling almost uncomfortable and prying to ask them. The feelings of unsurety, not knowing what will happen next.

But the strongest feeling is that of complete dependence on God. Although not really technically a feeling, it is so comforting to know that God is my Rock – I can lean on Him because He will always hold me up. Everything around me may be spinning out of control, all other securities may crumble and fall down, but God? He will always be by my side – He won't fail or let me down. He stands strong and firm. And that is so comforting.

Besides pray, they did what they could. They sent cards through the post, which I looked forward to and treasured. Every week they would call and hearing their voice would always bring warmth to my heart. I knew my mother found it hard that I, a mother of six children, was seriously ill, while she herself, of advanced age, was healthy. She told me once that she would gladly trade places with me. Mothers are special that way—their hearts are always beating for their children.

My cousin, Caroline, once shared with me how she was saddened that her mother was no longer alive at the time of her diagnosis and treatment. Someone once said to her that she must be relieved that her mother didn't have to witness what Caroline was going through. Nothing was further from the truth, and so Caroline replied, "I would give anything to have my mother here to walk beside me through this." Caroline missed her mother terribly, especially while enduring cancer.

We need our mothers. We need our fathers. We need their prayers, love, and support. They have been our constant companions and encouragers from birth. Now is not the time for that to change or waver.

I often wondered if I would ever become as old as my parents. Sometimes, I would even feel a fleeting pang of jealousy seeing older people that had lived for so many years. Time is a gift people receive in various measures and often don't appreciate its brevity or purpose. Is that what Moses meant when he wrote in Psalm 90:12 that we should number our days?

My parents-in-law, too, were amazing. Since they lived closer, about two hours away, they could provide considerable practical love and care. Often, the night before an operation, they would drive down and stay over. Not only did we find this greatly encouraging, it really helped the children to cope as well. Their "Oma" showered them with her love through her cooking and baking, and doing activities with them, providing as much stability as she could to their lives.

Your Siblings and Close Friends

Cancer binds, cancer separates, and cancer does all sorts of other things to relationships. Things happen that you may not expect to happen. Some will be pleasant, others not so pleasant.

I have six siblings, but only one that lived in Australia, about two hours away. He was a brother I had never been particularly close to. I had always tried to maintain some contact with him, but even that had fallen away in recent years. I had prayed for our relationship to flourish for longer than I can remember, but nothing seemed to change. In the end, I gave up praying about it.

Then I got cancer.

I still remember the day of his phone call. I was out in my garden, looking at my agapanthus plants that were flowering so beautifully alongside the shed, when my daughter came, holding the phone out to me. I answered it, and it was him. I was angry. I wanted to inflict pain. I wanted to make him feel like I had felt so often from his lack of consideration. So I lashed out: "If you're calling because I have cancer, don't bother." Wow, where had that come from? What had happened to the fruit of the Spirit that was supposed to influence my heart, and impact my speech? If our relationship wasn't in trouble before, it certainly was now. But I was in for a surprise. My brother didn't let my reaction thwart his purpose. He was going to be there for me, he said. He was going to make the changes needed.

Cancer does all sorts of things to relationships. Things happen that you may not expect to happen. Some will be pleasant, others not so pleasant.

Over the course of my cancer, my brother proved the validity of his words. He *was* there for me, time and again, emotionally, but most beautifully, spiritually—transparently so. My prayer for restoration had been answered, but in God's time and in God's way. Not in my time and in my way.

My other siblings, who all lived in Canada, also rallied to my support. None, bar one, had previously visited Australia, but by the end of the year of my treatment, every last one of them had touched down on Australia's red soil. Over the years I had desperately prayed that they would come and see where I lived and how I lived. I wanted them to get to know my husband better and meet my children. Once again, this prayer was answered in God's time and in God's way. I was beginning to realize that it was God who was ultimately in charge of these relationships in my life, and not me.

I couldn't help but wonder, as our house became a part-time hotel, what was their rush and motivation to traverse the globe and visit? I pondered how they were all processing and coping with my cancer diagnosis, while still living their normal day-to-day lives. They all came with such selflessness and an overwhelming urge to help, but was the fear of my death lurking underneath it all?

Whatever their motives, my siblings provided unending support to me. Phone calls, flowers, care packages, and emails all arrived with regularity. Their willingness to, each in turn, put their own lives on hold and fly across the world to help me and our family was of immense support. The spiritual sustenance I received through many of them was as much a blessing as their physical presence was. During the long nights of discomfort, nights when I couldn't sleep, nights when the clock seemed to move backwards, nights when everyone else in my household was asleep, I would call one of them, and, due to the time difference, they were still awake. I would ask them to read a Bible passage and pray with me over the phone. Those moments were precious moments, moments of beauty among the brokenness of disease.

Besides having siblings for friends, I have also been blessed with many other friends, all of varying personalities, all providing their own unique provisions to me. These were friends who stayed by my side through the thick-and-thin of cancer.

I had three friends in particular, friends that belonged to the same church as me, who consistently went the extra mile. They were unwavering in their love and support. God used them in mighty ways to provide for my needs during cancer. They all came with their own unique blessings. But, most importantly, they showed up, time and time again, when and where I needed them to.

When I read the book of Job I often smile, as he, too, had three friends. But mine were quite different from his. Nothing was too much for this "trio of blessings." My youngest child wasn't in school as yet and so would often need to be looked after when I went to all my appointments. Never was this too much. Eight loads of laundry to do on a Monday morning when I couldn't get out of my bed? Never was this a chore. Stopping by for a visit when I lived out of the way and the week was a busy one? Always had time. Needing my hair cut off? We'll be there in an hour to do it. Time to celebrate end of treatment at the beach? We'll bring the champagne.

My three friends could've written the book, *Just Show Up,*[18] they were so good at doing just that. God's love, time after time, was displayed clearly through them to me. I was so filled with gratitude at the grace He provided by means of these three that at the end of my treatment I threw them a "grace and gratitude" party. There, I read out a poem of thanksgiving I had written for the occasion:

I have three friends, all close to my heart
In different ways you have all left your mark
Your friendship was proven in the heat of trials
Always willing to go the extra mile

A telephone call, a gift, or a card
Your affection and love were never far
Out of comfort zones we all went
While endless prayers were heaven sent

---

[18] Tippetts and Buteyn, *Just Show Up.*

A brother's perspective . . .

The random phone calls from Helena, I think, impacted me the most. Helena up at all hours of her night. "Dave, I need someone to talk to and pray with and Andrew needs to sleep." We would talk about things that really matter in this life. First Helena would say that in spite of her cancer she knew that God is good and that He has a plan for her earthly life that would bring Him glory. (This is a very comforting theme that I also experienced with Caroline and others in their times of trial.) What could bring you through cancer if not the knowledge that God is good and that He loves us? Not just in times of sickness, but also through our entire lives here on this earth.

We talked and prayed many times together and Helena should know that as much as she thinks that it was me helping her through a particular bad spot, I would say the reverse was true. Seeing other people's faith in Jesus when bad things happen is a very humbling and faith strengthening experience.

The physical pain Helena was experiencing also came through over the phone and after one of the calls Annette said: "I think it's time we go and visit them." There she was, right in front of us in the Perth airport. Aside from the head scarf we wouldn't have known she was sick.

We didn't know what to expect but we thought we would be in for long days staying home with Helena, helping her around the house and such. Wow, were we wrong. From the moment we touched Australian soil it was go and go some more. Helena's energy just amazed us. I said to her at one point: "You know we could just hang out on your beautiful deck and read books." "Oh no," she said, "there's so much I need to show you" and off we went. We had a wonderful two weeks with Helena and Andrew and the kids. Picnics on the beach were the best.

Day two. Helena: "Um, today we have to go back to Perth for some tests." Off we went, not knowing what was in store. We sat on the sidewalk of a little café in Perth, Annette, myself, Andrew, and Helena having conversations that I refer to as way above my pay grade: Who makes life and death decisions? If God is in control, where does our will to live come into play? If the test is negative, does Helena stop treatment or does she persevere? Is it her decision alone, or is it made as a family? It is good that God is everywhere, even on a sidewalk café in Perth.

There is a lot more I could write about: Yallingup, Rottnest Island, and our final night with fish and chips on a blanket on the beach. We are very grateful for the time we had together.

In all of this we have got to know our Australian family much more intimately. I feel much closer to Helena as her brother but more importantly as a brother in Christ. Years ago I didn't hold that opinion, but God in His mercy has given us the opportunity, through something that seems bad to us, to turn it to our good. It is very comforting to me and my family to know that Helena moves ahead in her life fully trusting in Jesus to guide her home to glory at His appointed time.

Brother Dave

Nothing seemed too hard for any of you three
Better friends you could never be
As today we celebrate with Grace and Gratitude
I want you to know that I'm thankful, it's true

To have friends like you is from God above
An outpouring of His ever giving love
So let's celebrate together and praise Him for
All that He's given us through cancer's door

My friends couldn't fix everything. But they didn't have to. They weren't perfect. Then again, neither was I. But they were there. Every time. They did what they could (Mark 14:8).

I reminded myself not to limit my interactions with these three to solely what was going on in my world, as was easy to do. My friends still had their lives, their families, their concerns, and I was their friend as much as they were mine. I would try to reach out to them whenever I could. This is an important thing to remember when going through intense sufferings: it doesn't negate other people's struggles or other people's needs for friendship in return. Friendship is always a two-way street, although at times there is more traffic running in one direction than the other.

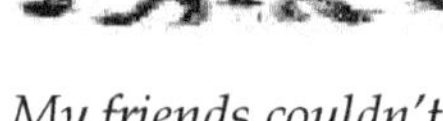

My friends couldn't fix everything. But they didn't have to.

But not every relationship was what it should have been. Unfortunately, it is not uncommon that during periods of affliction, friendships often suffer casualties. I was completely unprepared for this.

I have spoken to many people who have endured suffering, and their refrains are usually the same: although the operations, the treatments, the tiredness, and the physical pain are hard to bear, even harder was being hurt deeply by people they loved.

I have two very close childhood friends that I've known since I was about twelve years old. I just assumed they would both stand by me in my time of need. After all, we had gone through much of our lives together, had disclosed our hearts in great detail to one another during our school years, and had kept in touch with each other ever since. We were, as we had written in each other's high school yearbooks, "friends forever." Even thirty years after graduating, we had remained close. Needless to say, I was surprised at both their responses.

My one childhood friend reacted with anger—at me. She got angry that I had cancer, like it was my fault. The second childhood friend instantly and completely withdrew from my life.

Over the course of time the angry friend and I talked her feelings through. She soon returned to being a solid and loyal companion, doing what she could. Our friendship ended up deepening as a result. As for the other friend, I never heard from her again. I'm sure she has her side of the story. The problem is, I never got to hear it and was left hurt and confused.

My goal in sharing these relational excerpts is not so we can conduct a psychological analysis on why people react the way they do, or how a childhood friend could just walk away. They have their reasons. They may be reasons we don't understand. They may be reasons that aren't valid. They may be reasons that are valid, but ones we may not know about. Our prayer should be to give people the benefit of the doubt. And if we can't do that, we, at least, should forgive and extend mercy toward them. The destructive alternative is that we allow a bitter root to grow, which so easily happens in the bruised heart of the sufferer.

I was hurt deeply by some I loved as I went through cancer. You, too, may be hurting right now as a result of the actions or inactions of someone you love. But I began to see that people had to work through things in their own way and in their own time. And so, responses would vary, governed by many different things—the person's relationship with God, their ability to handle illness, their willingness to face the prospect of death, along with a myriad of other reasons that they probably don't fully understand themselves.

My husband, as well, experienced disappointments, although he was much more accepting of this occurring than I was. I suppose because I love my husband so much, I wanted those close to him to step up and be there for him. And some did, which was such a beautiful provision. But there was one hurtful exception, and I include this account so as to prepare you, my fellow sufferer, to deal with situations that cause pain in a biblical way and not a reactionary way. To be forewarned is to be forearmed.

This particular person pretended that nothing was happening out of the ordinary, that our circumstances hadn't changed, that our lives were completely normal. There was no elephant in the room that he saw. Naively, I thought the situation would improve once the shock of the initial diagnosis wore off. Surely, this person would see what we were going through. Surely, this person would stand by my husband through the storm, but, quite simply, it just didn't happen. Although my husband didn't struggle with this (I think he didn't have the same high expectations as I did), I did struggle. This person's conduct made me angry and so instead of me trying to understand the drivers behind the behavior, I was often infuriated by the behavior itself. It seemed that every time we were in a situation that provided an opportunity for him to reach out, nothing happened. In crucial times of sharing disappointing results, this individual would just pretend nothing was amiss. Fuel was continually added to the fire, resulting in deep-heated, repetitive pain.

I knew I had to release my anger and replace it with forgiveness, but I struggled to do so. After a while, I didn't want to let it go. It felt good to be angry at someone who appeared so unfeeling. I didn't want to understand there might be reasons governing his behavior. I just wanted my husband supported by him and was angry it wasn't happening.

But the anger started affecting me, and I knew I needed to deal with it before it got out of hand and I said things or did things I would live to regret. I knew anger and an unforgiving spirit went against the counsel of God and hindered my prayers. I knew that a bitter root was growing in my heart.

I spoke with my husband about my feelings, and also received some help from a wonderful counsellor who volunteered at Solaris. She provided a listening ear and objective counsel to people struggling through cancer. It was then that I first learned about the freezer. Yes, the freezer. You may have to learn about it too. You see, we know the Bible tells us that we must forgive—seventy times seven, in fact (Matthew 18:22). We also know that in our anger we must not sin (Ephesians 4:26). We know we have to overcome evil with good (Romans 12:21). But when fighting cancer, we're investing all our time and energy into getting through the days. There's not much left over. We need to use any strength we have on our relationship with God and our spouse and children and not pour it into energy sapping relationships. We can't change people when we're healthy and we certainly can't change them when we're sick!

And, so, this counsellor advised that if you have a relationship causing undue pain and have no energy to cope with it, to put the pain in the freezer and deal with it later. In fact, put the whole person in the freezer if you need to. Just freeze them out for the time being.

I'm not saying I completely agree with her advice. It's certainly not permission to permanently put people in the freezer—this is not the way of reconciliation and love that Scripture teaches. But when you are struggling to put one foot in front of the other, it may be helpful to deal with relational pain in this way for a time, with a view to restoration when the immediate pressure eases. This advice proved invaluable in my situation. Oh, there was still pain and anger. But it was more of a frozen pain and anger, one I could unthaw and process slowly as I regained energy, and one I eventually sought forgiveness for.

Thankfully, this challenging relationship was the exception rather than the rule. I needed many more suitcases to carry all the wonderful relational provisions God provided through family and friends than I needed freezers for those who just weren't able to be there for me or my family. Refuse to let the one or two people who cause you pain to negate all the other amazing care you receive—if anything, it makes the love of others shine even more brightly.

The diverse responses to suffering are undergirded by many things. Perhaps people can't face mortality—yours or theirs—which seemingly become intertwined in their minds. I accepted this more from those who didn't have hope for their eternities, but from Christians I found this response harder to understand. I suppose when they saw me it forced them to lift their gaze, currently preoccupied with the here and now, and face their own transience. The path of avoidance was much easier. It took some time for me to realize that they, too, were on a journey. People grow at different rates, also spiritually.

Unfortunately, understanding the possible explanations for people's behavior doesn't necessarily remove the hurt felt when people you expect to be there just aren't. I won't minimize this pain. Talk to anyone who has suffered. They've all had to bear this same cross, to one degree or another.

We can learn from each other. And so, if you are reading this, and you have a loved one that has cancer, or is suffering, be there for them. They need you. They need Christ's love through you. Don't add to their pain by not showing up or by employing avoidance techniques. It doesn't matter so much if you say the wrong thing or don't say anything at all. It doesn't matter if you cry and feel inadequate. It doesn't matter if you stare or are uncomfortable. What matters is that *you are there*. You're in the space, in the moment, in their life. You are sharing and caring, in your own unique way. We all have different roles to play in the body of Christ, but the key is to play them. Surrender your right

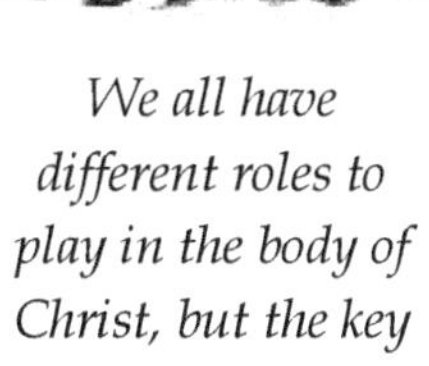

We all have different roles to play in the body of Christ, but the key is to play them.

to maintain control of the situation. That's not your job. Your job is to be there in the situation.

If you are weighed down under the burden of pain inflicted by someone you love being inexplicably absent in your season of suffering, do forgive. I know it's hard. At times, it's so hard you don't think you can. But it's Christ's way. Pray for help. Pray for those who inadvertently wound you. Love as you have been loved. Forgive as you have been forgiven (Matthew 18:21–35).

My diary entry written halfway through radiation shows the relational pain that was happening in my life, but also records the Spirit's response to my prayer for help in forgiving. This was a monumental day in my spiritual journey:

> Today I choose to forgive those who have said the most ridiculous things to me, some laughable, some ridiculous, and some downright hurtful. But the hardest ones for me to forgive are the absent ones—you know, the ones who you no longer see, or when you do, they pretend your life is normal. Help me to forgive as I have been forgiven. After all, I probably have done the same in my pre-cancer days.

Your Church Community

I was incredibly blessed to belong to a small country church community during the time I had cancer. I knew everyone well and they knew me. If there was anywhere to have cancer, it was here, in this lovely and loving rural church. Our families experienced births together, we had enjoyed years of Bible study together, had carpooled countless times together, had birthday parties together, and had basically done life together. We cared for one another as the body of Christ in that place. Don't get me wrong: it wasn't perfect. Nothing this side of heaven is. But it was pretty close.

Many times I felt this whole community (along with many other members of neighboring churches) praying for me, and travelling the road with me. Those times were grace injections that God provided to encourage me, carry me, and see me through. I remember several such occasions in particular:

- ♥ Receiving cards from the schoolchildren, all of them signing their names and making little drawings for me.

- ♥ Receiving close to two hundred cards from fellow pilgrims (not only from my local church, but also from other churches including ones from overseas) letting me know they were praying for me and my family. I hung every last one of these cards on the wall in our kitchen and it became known to our family as our prayer wall.

- ♥ Leaving the Lord's Supper table at church with tears in my eyes and having someone reach out and squeeze my hand as I returned to my seat.

- ♥ Opening my front door one morning and seeing four women standing there, dressed in red aprons that read: "Love, Peace, and Happiness." They worked all day, doing whatever needed to be done around the home.

- ♥ Having someone ring and ask if they could stop by with a delivery. That delivery turned out to be a handmade crocheted blanket, with many women having donated a square of their own design. I heard later that they had all prayed for me while crocheting their square.

- ♥ Having a woman who had a busy family drive an hour to our house to deliver a beautiful meal, and, when handing it over, saying: "It was nothing."

- ♥ Receiving homemade baking once a week from a mother who was very busy with her young children. The only week we didn't receive baking was when her oven broke down!

This was an amazing church community which shone out the love and care of Jesus Christ. Being part of a body of believers is an incredible provision. None of these believers could take my cancer away. They couldn't negate the effects of my treatment. But they could—and did—shower me with their love. I will always be grateful.

True, sometimes it was the ones you least expected to turn up that would be on your doorstep. Others that you may have expected to arrive may not have. But I was learning—learning to not judge books by their covers, learning, that God was busy in everyone's lives, learning that God would exalt the humble and humiliate the proud (Matthew 23:12), and how that was His job, not mine.

But in spite of all the prayers and love from my church community, there were still hard days. Like the day when the provision of my pastor and his wife was needlessly and painfully taken away from me. Then there were the days when I felt like a leper. The days when no one seemed to know what to say, or they'd become tired of saying it and just wanted things to go back to normal again, the same way I did. The days that were too confronting, like when I came to church wearing a scarf for the first time. I felt like the Red Sea had parted. It was difficult for everyone.

While you are suffering, realize that sensitivities are much higher than normal, and you don't always give the benefit of the doubt like you usually would. You may take offense much quicker than you typically would. Often you presume things that may not be true. This really struck me the day a friend came up to me after church. For months after my diagnosis she had avoided me. But today she didn't. She told me that every time she saw me, or I was prayed for in church, she would become very emotional, as it brought back memories of her mother having died of breast cancer. I hadn't known her mother had died of breast cancer. I learned a valuable lesson that day. Don't presume. Show grace. You don't always know the whole story.

It's not easy to support someone who is suffering. It's not easy to know what to say, what to do, what to write. But it also isn't easy suffering alone, or feeling like people are avoiding you. So always keep in mind that doing something is better than doing nothing.

When you do decide to say or write something, it's helpful to think about how it would feel if you were on the receiving end. For example, Bible verses are always comforting, but there is still a time and a place for their truths, and we need to be emotionally aware and pray for the Spirit to guide us as we impart the message of the Word.

It's not easy to support someone who is suffering. It's not easy to know what to say, what to do, what to write, but doing something is better than doing nothing.

One Scripture passage was particularly challenging for me, yet at the same time it was immensely comforting. It was none other than the text my son had framed for me: "And we know that all things work together for good to those who love God" (Romans 8:28 NKJV).

When you are going through hardships, this can be an extremely difficult text to read. It was a text that God was slowly bringing me to terms with. Yet, its truth couldn't be rushed, it couldn't be forced. Be aware that some Bible texts, although true and even comforting, might still be difficult to be on the receiving end of at certain stages of someone's journey.

The same goes for what you say. I once heard a story of a woman who was sitting in a chemo chair. A friend came to visit her. She patted her hand and said: "Now, now, God will be sure to turn this to your good." The woman ripped the needle out of her arm, held it out and said: "Here you go. Let Him turn it to your good, then!" I'm not sure if this is a true story. But it does teach us to be emotionally intelligent, even when quoting Bible verses. There is a time and a place for everything.

Having said that, the truth of Romans 8:28 did – in time – bring me immense comfort. God has to get the sufferer to this place and it doesn't happen overnight. The day will come when the afflicted will take the words of this beautiful confession on their lips. Others can't do it for them, can't push them to it. It requires time and refining. But one day, by the grace of God, those who have endured affliction can and will confess: "This was for my good."

Indeed, God is good and gives His children good things. When we have to deal with hard things as a result of the fall into sin or because of the devil's schemes, the wonderful truth is that God can and will turn them to the good of those who love Him. We may not always understand how this works out in our individual situations. But we need to believe the promise, because God always keeps His promises.

Part of God turning things to my good was my local church showering me with their love and care. These fellow pilgrims were a rich provision, living out the words of Romans 12:10–11, 15: "Be devoted to one another in love. Honor one another above yourselves. Never be lacking in zeal, but keep your spiritual fervor, serving the Lord. Rejoice with those who rejoice; mourn with those who mourn."

Your Medical Family

When I was diagnosed with cancer, I was thrown headlong into a world I never knew existed – the medical world. Oh, I had visited people in hospital before. I'd been to emergency with one child or another countless times. Now, it was different. The hospital became my home away from home. It felt like another world that I inhabited. The staff almost became my new family. Many of them, especially the ones I saw on a regular basis, became wonderful blessings in my life. Because it was their world, they understood mine. They understood when I winced when seeing a needle. They understood when a stray tear rolled down my face during chemo. They understood when I sat in the waiting room, waiting for results and hardly daring to breathe. They understood when I couldn't stand to look at myself in a mirror.

I was amazed at how many times the medical staff, whose job it was to do what they were doing, went so far beyond their call of duty. I wasn't just a patient to them. I was a person with a name, a person with a family, a person with a life, and they treated me as such. From the doctors to the nurses to the office staff to the cleaners, they understood what I was going through. I was deeply thankful for their provision of compassionate medical care.

Concluding Thoughts

To those of you who have family or friends that are suffering but you cannot find it within yourself to be there for them: I understand that it's hard. I understand that you wish this wasn't happening. I understand that this makes you face your mortality and you may not be ready for that. I understand you have reasons for reacting the way you do. I understand that you're way out of your comfort zone.

But what *you* need to understand is that you are adding to their pain by not being there for them. You may tell yourself you've been doing okay: you've been supporting them in prayer, you've been thinking about them a lot. But if you haven't actually been to see the person or spoken to them one-on-one, you are absent and may be causing pain in an already painful situation.

I pray that you receive the courage to follow in Jesus' footsteps (I know it's not easy). I pray that you follow the One who shone the love of God into so many hurting lives, and, that in His strength you go and do likewise. Don't hesitate or delay. Don't wait for Jesus to say: "Why have you been standing here all day long doing nothing?" (Matthew 20:6).

To the one being refined: You are walking a hard road. But when walking it, you must show grace to others along the way. You may think they should show grace to you and should overcome their fears and discomfort and support you. And many will. But some won't. You need to accept that. It is very important you don't let a bitter root grow in your heart because of it. This will only lead to more pain and place another burden on you to carry at a time when you are carrying quite a few burdens already. Focus instead on your relationship with God and getting through cancer. Focus instead on the relationships with people who are assisting and supporting you, especially those who are encouraging you in your walk with God.

You are walking a hard road. But when walking it, you must show grace to others along the way.

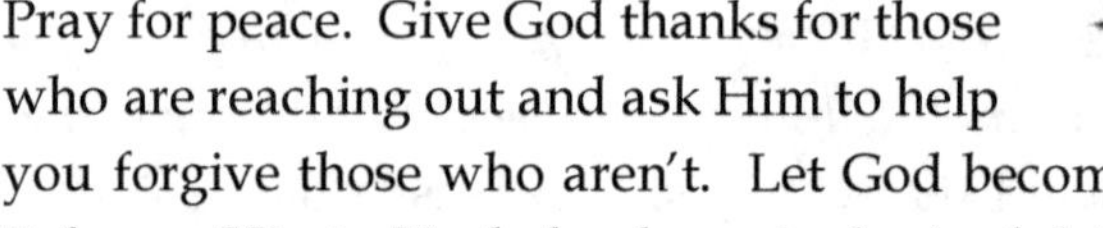

Pray for peace. Give God thanks for those who are reaching out and ask Him to help you forgive those who aren't. Let God become your everything. Rely on Him! He helped me to be joyful in hope, patient in affliction, and faithful in prayer. He will do the same for you.

The Triune God is our perfect Father, our perfect Brother, and our perfect Comforter. The Triune God is our perfect relational provision and chooses to dispense that provision through His image bearers, some who will shine His light brighter than others, some whose restoration is further along than others.

He perfectly carries out what He asks each one of us to do as we continually grow toward reflecting Him: to love sincerely and to be devoted to one another in that love.

Nine

The Mental Provision

Do not be anxious about anything.

PHILIPPIANS 4:6

I was used to living in a world of noise, with my brain whirling at maximum speed.

Having a busy family life and being something of a go-getter, my times of silence were few and far between. My mother spent a good part of her life encouraging me to slow down, often telling me I'm too busy. I'm not good at slowing down. I enjoy activity around me. But with cancer, my body was forced to slow down and all my busyness came to a grinding halt. My mind, however, continued to rush, no longer in sync with my body.

I had to slow my mind down and learn to be still. That was an adjustment—a good adjustment. By this point, a lot of my normal activities no longer seemed so important, anyways. What did become increasingly valuable was quiet time—time to spend in meditation and contemplation, looking at the bigger picture of life. I started to realize what I had been missing out on. I more and more began to treasure stillness and contemplation. This, in turn, allowed me the mental fortitude to cope with the rigors of cancer.

Activity now consisted of trips to appointments, trips to treatments, time on the couch or in bed recovering from operations, reading all the encouraging mail and emails, and reading all the books that had been stacked on my bedside table for a very long time, books I had been meaning to read, and now finally could.

Now that I had more times of silence, I had to learn to be comfortable in them and utilize them for good. I remember my cousin Caroline telling me that she would use quiet times to read the Bible and Christian books. I began to do the same. C.S. Lewis once described Satan and his demons as trying to make the world into a "Kingdom of Noise."[19] I felt I had truly escaped the din.

Slowing Down

With the peace came mental change. We read in Isaiah 30:15 that "in quietness and trust is your strength." I would wonder how that worked in the busy day-to-day of life. Everything I tried to do to slow down seemed to fail. Nothing ever seemed to work—until cancer.

Now here I was, quiet and restful, albeit at times against my will! This quietness gave God room to go to work. Unhurried meditation on God and His Word provided for intimacy with God that I hadn't known was possible. When I slowed my life down and savoured my most important relationship, I started growing ever closer to God. This deeper intimacy was vital for the mental fortitude required to navigate the roller-coaster ride of cancer. It wasn't that I hadn't experienced intimacy with God before. It wasn't that I hadn't spent time being still in His presence before. But having cancer, having many more opportunities to be still, allowed me access to a deeper connection. This was different than before, richer than before—like receiving special, spiritual food for an unprecedented part of my journey.

---

[19] Lewis, *The Screwtape Letters*, 121.

Turning Anxieties into Prayer

My quiet moments allowed me the time I needed to begin to unearth the destructive thought patterns creeping in, patterns that fuelled my anxieties. As I searched Scripture for answers on how to deal with these, I came across Philippians 4. Paul tells his readers not to be anxious about anything, but to pray and present their requests to God. Then, and only then, would God guard their hearts and minds with His peace (Philippians 4:6–7).

And so, when I felt anxious, I would pray over and over again for the peace of Christ to rule my heart. For help, to keep my eyes fixed above, to always bear in mind that God had a purpose and a plan and that He knew what He was doing. In the end, my mind seemed to become partitioned: there were mental pathways that were blocked, pathways that had stop signs in front of them. When I would find bitterness creeping in, I would arrest it. When I felt the presence of darkness, I would sing songs to keep evil at bay. When I was anxious about test results, I would pray and leave it with God.

When I felt anxious, I would pray over and over again for the peace of Christ to rule my heart.

Nevertheless, I still experienced times of despondency; times when pain would gain the upper hand and my tired mind would rediscover the closed paths. On the hardest days, days where I felt like God had brought me to the desert to die (Exodus 14:11), it would even be a battle to pray. I knew and believed that God would work things out for my good, but I wondered how long and arduous the journey would be. Like C.S. Lewis once wrote, "We are not necessarily doubting that God will do the best for us; we are wondering how painful the best will turn out to be."[20]

[20] Lewis, *Letters of C.S. Lewis*, 285.

As time progressed, my mental capabilities grew stronger and I tried not to worry about what was written on the next pages of my story. I only looked for strength for the page I was on at the moment. The peace of Christ began to overflow to become a peace with my circumstances, a peace with the pain that might lie along the way; a peace with not knowing what was around the next bend, a peace with not knowing how long the journey would be, and even, ever so slowly, a peace with how my husband and children would get through.

Guarding and controlling anxious thoughts, however, is not enough. Paul instructs God's children to go even further, replacing these thoughts instead with: "Whatever is true, whatever is noble, whatever is right, whatever is pure, whatever is lovely, whatever is admirable" (Philippians 4:8). God doesn't only want to curb the anxieties in my life; He wants my mind to be filled with lovely things! He wants me to see the beauty in the midst of the brokenness of the world around me.

Meditation

Meditating means thinking about something or someone deeply. Slowing down afforded the opportunity to meditate on God in a way that I never quite had before. This in turn allowed me to control what went on inside my head, as I drank deeply from the well of His Word.

My profoundest moments of intimacy occurred during such times of stillness in God's presence. This was when I mentally let go of all the stress and strain, when I took my eyes off myself and focussed instead on God—Who He was, His promises, and His plans. During this stillness, strong imagery, particularly as evoked by the poetic expression of the Psalms and the book of Isaiah, would often fill my thoughts. Imagery about hiding in the shelter of God's wings, imagery of dwelling in the light of His presence, imagery of soaring on wings of an Eagle, and imagery of the new earth, with its gold streets, and gates of pearl. At times I felt like I was breathing the very air of heaven.

The New Age movement, not surprisingly, have, for centuries, recognized these biblical truths as valuable. They understand the value of quiet, the value of meditation, the value of emptying your mind of anxieties, but they don't fill their minds instead with thoughts about the One and Only God of the universe. The New Age movement utilizes God-given directives to their own end—teaching the importance of meditation, mindfulness, and being in the moment; telling us about the need for stress reduction, inner peace, and harmony. Imparting truths we recognize, but wrapping them in a different spirit than the Life-Giving, Life-Changing Spirit who dwells in the hearts of believers.

Sadly, oftentimes Christians aren't utilising the gift of meditation to its full potential, not realizing the enormous blessings that result from it. If they utilized its full potential, it would change how they spent time with the LORD. It changed the way I did devotions in a significant way.

Scripture urges us repeatedly to meditate on God, (Psalm 1:2) to seek His face, (Psalm 105:4) to gaze upon His beauty, and spend time in His sanctuary (Psalm 27:4). But we're too busy, aren't we, crowding God out of our lives without even realizing it! We're starving for Him, but we don't take the time to feast at the table He spreads before us (Psalm 23:5). Are we too busy to realize how hungry we are? Is that why God brings events that trigger a hunger for Him into our lives? Deuteronomy 8:3 reads: "He humbled you, *causing you to hunger* and then feeding you with manna" (emphasis mine).

There was a place called Solaris Cancer Care near my hospital. They provided complementary cancer therapies for those going through treatment. It was a house that had been converted into a type of retreat. You could enjoy a stress-relieving massage, do some meditation, or simply relax in their comfortable recliner chairs, all for free. It was a beautiful place, staffed by compassionate volunteers, and I loved going there for respite. It was there that I could really let go mentally of all the stress and strain and instead meditate on God.

While Solaris was not overtly New Age, I knew that not all cancer patients meditating there were meditating on God. If only that were true! I used their principles of slowing down and being in the moment, not to guide me to look for strength in myself, but rather to show me that my strength lay in God's strength. He was leading me beside quiet waters, using these times to restore my soul. In this way I used my visits to Solaris to meditate on the One that mattered, the One equipping me to walk on, ready to face whatever cancer could throw at me, in the knowledge that the joy of the LORD was my strength (Nehemiah 8:10).

Music

Just as C.S. Lewis thought hell would be a place of discordant noise, he contrasted heaven as being filled with jubilant music. He explains that there is beauty to be found in many things, including music, but this is only because things such as music show up the longing for what we truly desire: "For they are not the thing itself; they are only the scent of a flower we have not found, the echo of a tune we have not heard, news from a country we have never yet visited."[21]

I had always loved music and had been active in community radio for many years. Now that I had cancer, music came to play even a bigger role in my life, and I used this to great advantage. I had more playlists in our home than anyone else. I had playlists for everything: "Mom's treatment playlist," "Mom's recovering playlist," "Mom's meditative playlist" and many others. Even my daughters couldn't compete!

The Psalms, as put to Genevan music, were my top favorites, as they conveyed the message of the one hundred and fifty biblical Psalms so faithfully and beautifully. These were Psalms I had known from my youth. During many a worship service, the words of these Psalms would get stuck in my throat because they

[21] Lewis, *The Weight of Glory*, 5.

reminded me of God's presence and promises in powerful, visceral ways, and, as such, evoked a strong emotional response.

Sons of Korah,[22] an Australian Christian band, combine the words of the Psalms with deeply emotive music. I had always enjoyed listening to them, and now did so more than ever. In the middle of my cancer journey my husband and I went out with some good friends to one of their concerts. I remember them playing Psalm 121—a Psalm I often reflected on as I looked out on the hills of our property. But as their concert drew to a close, it appeared as if they were not going to play another favorite I had been hoping for—Psalm 91, a Psalm I was in the process of memorizing. It was a Psalm that had become very dear to both Caroline and me, and we had often talked about how beautifully comforting its message was. She, too, often listened to Sons of Korah's music to help her find peace.

Imagine how I felt when the evening ended up concluding with none other than Psalm 91! What a consoling provision God gave to me through the Sons of Korah's music.

Sometimes when listening to other Christian artists I could tell by their song lyrics that they, too, had walked through the fire and discovered God's provisions there. For example, a friend of mine once recommended Laura Story to me, and as I listened to her *Blessings* CD,[23] shortly after my first operation, I thought to myself: "She's had cancer, otherwise she couldn't write and sing the way she does." Some time later, when reading her CD cover, I discovered I wasn't far off the mark—her husband had suffered a brain tumour. You recognize the refining, I suppose, of fellow travellers. Her song, "Blessings,"[24] really spoke to my soul, encouraging me that even though things seem bad, they are working for good.

---

22 Sons of Korah is a Christian band founded in 1994 in Geelong, Victoria, Australia. It takes its name from the biblical family of the same name. The band is known for putting Psalms to music. The lyrics for their songs are taken almost verbatim from the Bible book of Psalms.

23 Laura Story, *Blessings*.

24 Laura Story, "Blessings," Track 5 on *Blessings*.

Books

I had always loved reading, but never seemed to have enough spare time for it. During cancer, books became precious mental provisions for me. Works I had enjoyed before now found me appreciating them anew, this time with a vested interest. I tremendously enjoyed the works by saints who had gone before—writers such as C.S. Lewis, Charles Spurgeon, J.C. Ryle, and Corrie ten Boom. There were also current authors I found valuable: Ann Voskamp (*One Thousand Gifts*), Paul D. Wolfe (*My God is True!*), and Joni Eareckson Tada (*Joni*), to mention but a few.

One particular book that encouraged me to persevere was *Suffering and the Sovereignty of God*,[25] a book written by several Reformed authors, all contributing their own personal stories of suffering interpreted through the lens of Scripture. Reading books such as this widened the horizon of my mind and brought perspective on the greater picture of what God was doing both on a global scale and also in my life. Reading about other Christians' journeys and their testimonies of how God saw them through protected me from self-pity. I saw that others had struggled with so much more than I, and that God had been faithful to them and had helped them to cope. Their retelling of God's marvelous deeds in their lives gave me assurance for my own life, reminding me of His promises that He would do the same for me.

By far, though, the most beautiful Words I read were the Words from God Himself. His Words of Life brought me time and again into mental green pastures. There, I was able to be filled with hope and peace. I drank deeply from the Rivers of Life that flowed every time I opened its pages.

Processing

As events would unfold quite rapidly at times, it was difficult to maintain mental equilibrium. I had to have time and space to process my thoughts. My husband was such a blessing to me in

[25] Piper et al., *Suffering and the Sovereignty of God.*

this regard, always making sure I had the moments and the places to sort out in my mind what was happening in my life. Somewhat unintentionally, we fell into a pattern. We would go to the hospital to obtain results of tests or surgeries and afterward we would drive directly to the home of our pastor and his wife. Providentially, they lived very close to the hospital. They would always stand ready to read the Bible and pray with us. (This couple was one of God's greatest relational provisions to us.)

Next, we would go to a café by the beach, just the two of us, and have a coffee to further digest the latest news and explore one another's feelings and emotions. Then finally, we would go home to tell our children. Usually the following day we would write an email to family, friends, and the church community. This pattern became our method of managing the incredibly draining process of mentally absorbing, processing, and sharing the results that the frequent tests and operations brought.

From time to time, my husband thoughtfully arranged nights away for just the two of us. This allowed the opportunity to remove ourselves physically from cancer's heartbeat, to give ourselves moments where we could just have some fun. Sometimes it simply allowed us the privacy to collapse and bear the weight of the burden with no one else around. Some close friends most thoughtfully gifted us a weekend away at a bed and breakfast in the countryside, during a time of heightened anxiety. This proved to be of immense assistance in maintaining our mental fortitude and was a very thoughtful way for them to extend the love of Christ.

Going out for a cup of coffee, going for a walk on the beach, or enjoying an early morning run—these were all moments that were important in ensuring that a mental backlog would not slow us down in running the race.

One Day at a Time

My pastor, shortly after I was diagnosed, gave me some very simple advice on how to cope mentally. "Take things a step at a time," he said. "There's no point worrying about walking through door number eight, when door number three is right ahead. That's the door you need to walk through today. Who knows? You may never have to walk through door number eight, anyways! So why worry about it now?" Indeed, Jesus tells us this same thing Himself in Matthew 6:34: "Do not worry about tomorrow, for tomorrow will worry about itself. Each day has enough trouble of its own." How true. Just like the Israelites were to collect manna for that day only and not gather for the next day (Exodus 16:4), so we receive God's strength for each day, with His mercies new each morning (Lamentations 3:23).

Living a day at a time eases mental strain. Sometimes you may even have to take it an hour at a time. When you're lying awake at night in pain thinking you can't stand it any longer, and the clock on the wall is going backward, take it a minute at a time. Don't let your thoughts go past the present. Mentally, it is more than you can bear. Try not to worry about things like whether you will be alive when your son gets married. Instead, focus on getting through the next six hours of the night. Let that be enough. After all, who of us by worrying can add one extra hour to our lives? (Matthew 6:27).

Mental Capability

Why do some Christians appear to handle cancer journeys (or other major life-altering events) relatively well, while others seem to crumble? This is a complex and multifaceted phenomenon, especially when you consider that body and soul are inextricably linked. As such, it's a question I can only partially address, perhaps the observations made being of some help.[26]

Some say it is all a matter of spirituality. If your faith is strong enough, you'll receive the mental provision from God to cope. Others will focus on physical attributes and will say that if you are in good physical shape, you will bounce back easier. Still others

---

[26] It is beyond the scope of this book to explore neuroplasticity—how the brain continually transforms itself in response to pain and experiences, either in a positive or negative way.

say those with good relational support will cope better. Personal character, say others, surely plays a role. If you have a persevering character, a fighting character, this will enable you to push through mental and physical barriers easier than others.

While all of these have a ring of truth to them, all of them are in and of themselves too simplistic an answer. Take spirituality. If you have a strong faith in God, shouldn't you be able to weather any storms God brings your way? How about a storm such as mental health? Both Martin Luther and Charles Spurgeon are examples of men with great faith who still experienced considerable mental anguish.

What about two people who have been in a serious car accident? One may bounce back with a "I'm going to survive" mentality and end up becoming a marathon runner five years later, while the other can be found curled up in a ball, scared to face the outside world. Can you really attribute their reactions to one having more faith than the other? I don't think there is a "one size fits all" answer. Instead of focussing on what we don't know, let's look at what we do know. God tells us: "My grace is sufficient for you, for my power is made perfect in weakness" (2 Corinthians 12:9).

God will give us mental provisions as He sees fit. The scope of these provisions may vary according to His perfect wisdom and His perfect plan. Their effectiveness depends in part in how we responsibly utilize the provisions He supplies. That may look different for different people in different situations with different character attributes who are at different points in their spiritual growth. The bottom line is that God does give the provisions we need for our journey, and we are to responsibly make use of them.

Humor

Some people use humor to provide a bit of mental release, and I would witness this in hospital waiting rooms now and again. While it may be helpful for some, it's not for everyone, and, to be honest, it wasn't for me. I think my brother, who witnessed one such episode, would agree. One day, while waiting for me to return from a PET scan, he observed another woman waiting for her turn. While she waited, she was joking with the receptionist at the clinic counter. My brother—who, by the way, is normally the first to crack a good joke—just couldn't understand this. He said to me later: "How could she laugh at a time when so much was at stake?"

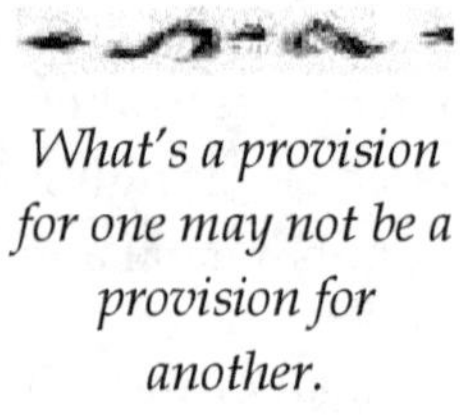

What's a provision for one may not be a provision for another.

What's a provision for one may not be a provision for another. If you wish to use humor as a mental distraction for someone who is suffering, make sure it will be welcomed.

Information Overload

When I was diagnosed, I read everything I could get my hands on about cancer. Soon, I found out that it was possible to read too much, to search too much, and to know too much.

Some people need to know everything. Some people don't want to know anything. I fell in between these two groups. I wanted to understand what was going on with my body. I wanted to be able to converse with my medical team in an intelligent, proactive manner. But being overly inquisitive can rob you of the peace of Christ and can also cause you additional mental stress. It can even cause you to think that cancer has to follow the rules you've uncovered in what you've read, tempting you to forget that it is ultimately God Who is in charge of the situation.

In the end, I settled on referring to two good medical books, one helpful natural remedies book, perused two helpful websites, and kept my Bible by my side. That was enough information for me!

Normal Routines

It was good for my mental state—and also for my children's—that I continued to maintain as much of my normal routine as I could. I kept going to the gym, I kept jogging around the block, and I kept being an active member on our local school council. (They were so supportive, while at the same time never pitying me.) I tried to cook whenever I could and be there for my children whenever possible.

I also continued with presenting my Sunday night radio program, called *Evensong*. This was a wonderful opportunity to process mentally what was happening in my life, to verbalize events and put them into a spiritual framework. I wonder if my listeners realized that my meditations and music selections were probably feeding my soul more than theirs!

Going to church twice a Sunday and Bible study during the week, as I had always done, not only fed me spiritually, but was important for my children, as it meant I was doing things Mom had always done.

It wasn't always possible to continue normal routines, especially during times of treatment, but I tried to maintain some of them nonetheless. I tried to be there when my children got home from school. I tried to be there when they had soccer games or participated in music performances. I tried to swim in the pool with them, or play a bit of cricket.

I encourage you, for your sake, but also for the sake of your husband and children, to continue to do as much as you possibly can. There are times when your limitations are real, and you simply can't. That's understandable. That's fine. I had plenty of those moments. But there will be other times where you may be susceptible to self-pity. Fight those times. Get up and go for that walk. Put on your headscarf and go shopping for school supplies. Read that book to your child on the couch. Go to your son's game. Drive your daughter to music lessons. Go on a date with your husband. Whatever you are able to do, do it! It will help your mental state, and the mental state of your family.

Above all, ask God to help you remain mentally strong. He will do it all for you, but never without you. You can do all things through Him who gives you strength. He will meet all your needs—including your mental needs—according to the riches of His glory in Jesus Christ.

Ten

The Emotional Provision

Trust in the LORD with all your heart
and lean not on your own understanding;
in all your ways submit to Him,
and He will make your paths straight.

PROVERBS 3:5–6

I'm an emotional person—at least, I always had been. My mother would tell me that when I was young I cried after most of my birthday parties. Perhaps it was in order to release tension. My highs were high and my lows were low. Even as an adult, if I read a sad book, tears will undoubtedly stain its pages. If I'm watching a dramatic movie, you will hear a sob or two during poignant scenes. A sermon in church, or even attending the Lord's Supper, will often result in watery eyes. And so, when I received my cancer diagnosis, I thought: I'm going to dissolve into an emotional wreck! My family, surely, were drawing their own, similar conclusions.

But I hadn't counted on God's intervention, on God's emotional provision to me. Looking back, I am amazed that, although I certainly experienced times of instability during my cancer journey, overall, never had I felt in such control of my emotions.

There was no way I could attribute this emotional strength to myself. God's power was on display in my life, and I could only stand by and be thankful for His provision of stability.

Reflecting on the place of emotions, and identifying the role they played in the lives of biblical characters, increased my understanding of the place they should hold in the life of a Christian. God had taught me lessons about this at other times, but, now, He was forcefully driving them home. Maybe this was what C.S. Lewis meant when he said: "God whispers to us in our pleasures, speaks in our conscience, but shouts in our pains: it is His megaphone to rouse a deaf world."[27] God was shouting, and I was listening.

Emotions evoke in us strong feelings derived from our circumstances, and often are "accompanied by physiological and behavioral changes."[28] These feelings, although important, are subjective, and need to be recognized as such.

Subjecting Emotions to Truth and Obedience

Emotions are hard to define. There's a lot we don't understand about them. But we do know that they are created by God and serve an important function. They color our lives, making us the unique individuals we are. Different individuals express and deal with their emotions in different ways. Some seem to be governed by them, others don't seem to have them. Some seem to control them, others give themselves over to them with reckless abandon.

Emotions can be irrational. Surprising. Unreliable. Beautiful. Heartfelt. Powerful. Our feelings vary, based on many things—the weather, health, our stress levels, the amount of sleep we've had and many other factors. But no matter what our emotions might be, they must be supported by the foundation of truth and obedience.

---

[27] Lewis, *The Problem of Pain,* 91.

[28] *Merriam-Webster Dictionary,* s.v. "emotion."

Now this doesn't negate the validity and existence of our emotions, but it does make us realize that they should not be elevated to a place where they don't belong. Our emotion-focused culture leads us to believe that emotions are truth, that because you feel something, it must be true, making emotions and truth interchangeable. But they are not one and the same. Emotions should never be elevated over Truth, because emotions are unreliable. God's Truth, found in His Word, isn't.

Emotions should never be elevated over Truth, because emotions are unreliable. God's Truth isn't.

In the Bible, the Holy Spirit uses the descriptions of emotions as a conduit to understanding God's reactions to situations. However, God's "emotions" are always to be viewed through His perfect character traits of love, mercy, wisdom, sovereignty, to name a few. God's "emotions" are never outbursts, but instead are always a perfectly controlled and executed expression of His wisdom.

As His image bearers, we need to learn how to rightly express and handle our emotions in a God-pleasing way. His Son, Jesus Christ, gave us many examples of how to do just that. The Bible speaks of Jesus as being deeply distressed, troubled, and overwhelmed with sorrow (Mark 14:33–34) when He was in Gethsemane. He also felt righteous anger (John 2:15–16). These were but a few of Jesus' emotions. What sets His emotions apart was that they were always borne out of truth and obedience, and so never caused Him to sin.

Unfortunately, the same can't be said of us. For example, if we are going through a difficult time, our emotions might tell us that God is distant and doesn't care about us and what we are going through, even though the Bible gives us a different and truth-filled answer. As a result, we may tend to pull away from God, to freeze Him out of our hearts. We may be tempted to amputate our perceived source of pain, which in turn leads us to disobedient rebellion against God.

We often don't control our emotions, don't subject them to the truth of the Bible. We don't subject them to the promises God has made to us, we don't subject them to past experiences where God has done great things for us. We let our hearts overrule the truth of the Word and so often end up sinning with our emotions by being wise in our own eyes (Proverbs 3:7).

We need to enlist the help of the Holy Spirit to enable us to train our emotional responses so they are in line with the truths of Scripture. Truth needs to be the locomotive of our lives, guiding and pulling us and our emotions forward in obedience. If we allow "emotion" to become the locomotive, pulling truth behind it, we can derail our lives.

If our emotions contradict Scripture's truth, these are times we must bend the knee and cry out to God in prayer. These are the times when we need to grab hold of God's promises with both hands. These are the times when all our years of memorizing the truths contained in Scripture will bring us to a place of remembrance, will bring us to a place of subjecting our emotions to known truths. In this way, we can walk forward in the way of Truth, in the path of obedience, trusting in God and not leaning on our own understanding.

The people of Israel, about to enter the Promised Land of Canaan, were fearful of having to fight the inhabitants of the land. Their leader, Moses, reminded them to subject these fears to God's promises: "Be strong and courageous. Do not be afraid or terrified because of them, for the LORD your God goes with you; He will never leave you nor forsake you" (Deuteronomy 31:6).

There is but one source of truth—the Word of God. God's Word and promises are sure and firm and completely trustworthy. Our emotions aren't. As creatures created with emotions, we need to subject our emotion to what God tells us, to what God does for us. We must be led to the Rock of refuge that is higher than us, time and time again (Psalm 61:2), anchoring ourselves to that Rock, in the security that God will ensure it will not give way in the stormy sea of emotion.

The Psalms also provide many examples of how to submit our emotions to the truths of the Word. Psalm 116 is but one poignant example: "The cords of death entangled me, the anguish of the grave came over me; I was overcome by distress and sorrow. Then I called on the name of the LORD: 'LORD, save me!'" (vs 3–4). King David was overwhelmed with anguish in this Psalm. But look what happens. He subjects his emotions to the truth of God's Word and so concludes, not with being overwhelmed, but being at rest: "Return to your rest, my soul, for the LORD has been good to you" (v7). King David subjected his emotions to truths he knew about God. We need to learn to do the same.

Deuteronomy 6:5 reads: "Love the LORD your God with all your heart and with all your soul and with all your strength." The emotion of love needs to be undergirded by the truth of God's Word and an obedience to that Word. Love without obedience is not really love. Loving God also means living an obedient life. Jesus says in John 14:15: "If you love me, keep my commands." Tapping into emotional love may be easy. But God asks us to love with more than our hearts. Our souls and minds, too, have to be resolute on covenant obedience to Him.

Specific Emotions

Worry

Let's look at the emotion of worrying. Matthew 6:27 reminds us: "Can any one of you by worrying add a single hour to your life?" Worrying about test results, worrying about how we will get through chemotherapy, worrying about whether we will live or die, worrying about how our families will cope without us are all things people with cancer can easily do. All this worrying, though, doesn't actually change a thing. The only thing it may start to change is our trust in God, making us doubt that God has all this under His sovereign, wise, and loving control.

Instead of worrying, Philippians 4:6 has these words of instruction: "Do not be anxious about anything, but in every situation, by prayer and petition, with thanksgiving, present your requests to God." Don't be anxious. Instead, pray! Give thanks! Then let the peace of God placate your worries.

Fear

Fear is a very real emotion for cancer patients. Fear about the future, fear about upcoming test results, fear about impending pain. It's not easy to let scriptural truths overcome fear. But with the Spirit's help, it is achievable.

You may need to memorize Scripture. You may need to write Bible verses on sticky notes and put them on your mirror, on the dash of your car, on your fridge, on your cancer file. But whatever you do, take God's truth with you into every fearful situation. Scriptures such as the one we find in Isaiah 41:13 can combat fear in a most powerful way: "For I am the LORD your God who takes hold of your right hand and says to you, Do not fear; I will help you." Don't let your fearful emotions get the upper hand over the truths found in God's Word.

Anger

Sometimes anger can be used as an emotional outlet—anger toward anything or anyone that is causing us pain or frustration, anger toward others for not understanding and supporting us, even anger toward God for "letting this happen."

The Bible is not silent here. Anger is not listed as a fruit of the Spirit (Galatians 5:22–23), but self-control is. And so, Ephesians 4:26–27 warns us: "'In your anger do not sin': Do not let the sun go down while you are still angry, and do not give the devil a foothold."

Joy and Peace

Subjecting our emotions to God's truth doesn't mean life will always be easy. It doesn't mean that, at times, our emotions won't overwhelm us. But it does mean that in the face of these strong emotions, we can still be filled with joy and peace, powerful realities that are undergirded by powerful spiritual truths. These truths give us perspective and widen our gaze to the bigger picture God is revealing in and through our fear and pain. This is peace that transcends our emotions and transcends all understanding (Philippians 4:7).

That this perspective gives us joy is not as far-fetched as you may think. Listen to the apostle Peter, an apostle known for frequently letting his emotions get the upper hand:

> In all this you greatly rejoice, though now for a little while you may have had to suffer grief in all kinds of trials. These have come so that the proven genuineness of your faith—of greater worth than gold, which perishes even though refined by fire—may result in praise, glory and honor when Jesus Christ is revealed. Though you have not seen Him, you love Him; and even though you do not see Him now, you believe in Him and are filled with an inexpressible and glorious joy, for you are receiving the end result of your faith, the salvation of your souls (1 Peter 1:6–9).

Whenever we suffer, we need to instruct our accompanying emotions to the truth that this suffering is there to refine us. Although we may sow with tears from these trials, we will one day reap with songs of joy (Psalm 126:5).

The joy we reap doesn't lie *in* the pain and suffering itself, but the joy lies in knowing God has a plan *with* our pain and suffering, a plan that will culminate with the harvesting of our souls. It's a plan which will result in His glory and our good. It's a plan that continually demonstrates God's love to us, a plan which cost God His One and Only Son. A plan that gives joy amidst tears, a plan that gives you peace amidst the turbulence, a plan that displays beauty in the brokenness. A plan that is unfolding in your life right now.

And, so, each one of us can have joy and peace in our journeys as we travel from this temporal existence toward the eternal one, irrespective of what the journey holds, knowing that the path each one of us is on is God-ordained. He will make your path straight. It may not be the path we would have chosen, but it is the path that is needed to make us what we must become. And so, as we walk through the desert of suffering, we receive our Guide's emotional provisions along the way: "You will keep in perfect peace those whose minds are steadfast, because they trust in You" (Isaiah 26:3).

Remember and Believe

It's not always so easy, this subjecting of our emotions to truth and obedience. We read about the people of Israel—hungry and thirsty as they travelled, constantly complaining to Moses—and we think: what a bunch of complainers! Don't they remember that God divided the Red Sea for them? Don't they remember that God rescued them from slavery? Don't they remember the plagues of Egypt? Can't they control their emotional outbursts, realizing the truth of Who God is and being obedient to Him as they travelled?

But are we really any different? Do we stop and remember what God has done for us in the past? Or do we, too, allow our current situation and its accompanying emotions to override these remembrances? The Bible often instructs God's people to recall the things of the past, because these recollections give confidence for the future. These remembrances display that God is true to every single last promise He has made. This is exactly what the distressed Asaph does in Psalm 77:11–12: "I will remember the deeds of the LORD; yes, I will remember your miracles of long ago. I will consider all your works and meditate on all your mighty deeds."

God taught me the importance of submitting my emotions to His truth. He accomplished this by opening His Word to me, feeding me, and reminding me of these truths throughout the hard moments and emotions of the day. Through His Spirit, God called to mind many other instances in my life where He had been beside me, giving me all I needed. Why should things be any different today?

Walk on, dear pilgrim, knowing that the straight path God has marked out for you will lead to your heavenly country. Use the streams of living water He provides along the way to assuage any emotions that threaten to overtake. Drink deeply from this stream and remember the truths you have been taught from His Word and what He has done for you in the past. Write them on the tablet of your heart and trust the Lord, knowing that His grace is sufficient for His power is made perfect in weakness (2 Corinthians 12:9).

Go your way in safety, submitting your emotions to God's truth. Walk in obedience, in trust, knowing your foot will not stumble. Then you won't be afraid when you lie down, for the LORD will be at your side.

Eleven

The Physical Provision

Do you not know that your bodies are temples of the Holy Spirit?

1 CORINTHIANS 6:19

Cancer shouldn't have happened to me, if the statistically derived risk factors were anything to go by. I was very healthy. I ate well, went to the gym, and generally looked after my body. I avoided using chemicals in the home and, as much as the family budget allowed, ate organic, and checked my meat sources closely. I tried to buy local and home-grown produce where I could.

Not only did I take good care of my body, I was also quite protective of it. My body was God's workmanship and I wanted that workmanship left intact. I didn't like it being manipulated, changed, or scarred. This manifested itself in all sorts of ways. For example, I avoided needles. When I go to the dentist I refuse to have anaesthetic, rather enduring the pain. My chiropractor bemoans the fact I can't relax when he needs to manipulate my neck. I know it must be done, but I like my body being left alone. I'm quite stringent in not allowing toxins into my body, and even have an aversion to swallowing paracetamol for a headache, unless absolutely necessary. This protective stance also means I struggle with going to the doctor, in spite of knowing it is their job to care for my earthly tent, and it is a job they carry out with utmost professionalism.

All this did not bode well for my cancer journey. Countless operations, countless examinations, countless needles, and countless treatments all became a regular part of my life, and I didn't like any of it. My well-protected body was being attacked by cancer cells and these cells in turn had to be attacked with surgical knives, poisonous substances, and damaging radioactive waves. Evil had to be fought with evil, and there was nothing I could do about it.

Could it be that my thirst for perfection in a broken world played a role in my protective mindset—that I wanted things to be as close to their original state of created perfection? Most likely, it did. Here, too, I had to realize that bodily perfection was something that lay ahead and was not something I could possess perfectly this side of eternity.

On the other hand, I knew I needed to honor God with my body, that I had to be a good steward over it, and so I began to pray for His help and guidance in how best to care for it through the rigors of cancer.

Conventional versus Natural Treatment

The primary decision to be made was whether to embrace conventional cancer treatments or opt, instead, for the myriad of natural remedies on offer. Investigating both options was like walking through a minefield. Was there anything to the pharmaceutical company conspiracy theories? Did dandelion root really cure cancer? If it did, why were the chemo wards still full of people? Should I be buying the latest juicer on the market and drink vegetables all day long? How about taking vitamin C capsules before chemo?

Soon, I became completely overwhelmed. Very well-intentioned friends and even strangers all shared their opinions on how cancer could be treated and cured, and I no longer knew what to think or do. Once, as my husband and I were in the waiting room before one of my surgeries, a documentary on television interviewed a woman who had had cancer in her arm bone and the doctors had recommended amputation. This woman chose to go on a strict diet instead and—guess what? She was cured! Yet here I was, minutes away from amputation! Information overload from countless sources resulted in this being a very confusing time.

Where did we begin? How were we going to make the hard decisions? We prayed for wisdom and guidance, but the Bible doesn't tell us if I should use chemotherapy or drink pawpaw leaf tonic. But God's Word does tell us that He will give wisdom to those who ask (James 1:5). So we asked, and waited on God to be true to His promise to give us wisdom as we sought out treatment options.

One day, while at Solaris Cancer Care waiting for my massage, I came across a book on their library shelf. It was written by a naturopath who shared many of the same concerns about caring for your body through cancer and its treatments. Upon her cancer diagnosis, she completed extensive research into both conventional and natural treatment methods. To cut a very long book short, she concluded that although conventional treatments were paramount to combatting cancer, she would do everything possible to combat their negative effects using natural antidotes and so allow the body to bounce back as quickly and strongly as possible.

After much soul searching, discussion, receiving godly counsel, prayer, and reading (including the book from the naturopath), we came to the conclusion that the pathway the doctors recommended was a vital part of God's care and provision over me. This helped us to accept the necessity of receiving conventional treatments, treatments including surgery, chemotherapy, and radiation. At the same time, we were highly cognizant of the

Our prayers for wisdom were answered, and we went forward with peace in our hearts.

goodness of the many natural remedies that God had placed in His creation which could only help my body.

And, so, our prayers for wisdom were answered, and we went forward with peace in our hearts, using the physical provisions God so graciously supplied.

Diet

Early on in my cancer journey, I began reading a lot about diet. A lady from our church visited and explained about foods and the dangers inherent in coloring and preservatives. Many others also read and investigated diet options and shared their results with me.

I became somewhat relentless in my focus on diet, while at the same time realizing that I couldn't do everything I wanted to do. After all, I had a husband and six children to care for and feed, and a budget to meet. Reality had to make an appearance in our menu choices. I tried to use common sense in deciding what to pursue and what to leave out.

In the end, I completely cut out sugar, as there seemed to be some evidence of it possibly "feeding" cancer. Cutting out sugar also meant cutting out carbohydrates and I even avoided fruits high in natural sugars.

However, cutting out certain foods was only the beginning. I vastly increased my intake of healthy foods, especially greens. I ate them, cold-pressed them, and drank them. Adding as many greens into the family dinner menu as possible did not go unnoticed by our children. My son asked some of his friends over for dinner one night, and I overheard him warning them they would probably be eating broccoli if they stayed. Later on, his friends said to him: "You weren't kidding." Broccoli soup, broccoli salad, and broccoli fish casserole had all been on the menu that evening!

When my bear of a brother from northern Canada visited, I took him along on my weekly shopping expedition to our local farmer's market. As he unloaded the cartload of vegetable produce at the checkout, this lumberjack of a brother looked at me aghast and said: "I never thought it would be possible to fill up a trolley with so much green stuff! Are we really going to eat all of that?"

My tastebuds started to change. I began craving things like grapefruit (something I could never eat before) and could no longer tolerate anything with sugar. I lost weight as a result, but could tell my body loved the care I was giving it.

Exercise

I had always been aware of the importance of exercise and wasn't going to let cancer change this. I continued to work out at the gym and go running with my husband. He had taken up running together with me when the first effects of my treatments had started, perhaps to make sure I was going to be all right. There was no more beautiful place to run than in the rural hamlet in which we lived. Running first thing in the morning, with the sun creeping over the hills, was not only a physical experience, but also a deeply spiritual one for me. It wasn't just good for my body, but it was also good for my soul.

It's no surprise, then, that my second question to my surgeons (after asking them when I could go home) would always be: "When can I begin exercising again?" I would start as soon as I was allowed, sometimes earlier if I felt up to it. There were times when I would have to skip the intense group fitness sessions, times I would have to lower my weights, and times I couldn't run my normal distances. Exercise enabled my body to recover swiftly and I'm convinced it prevented long-term effects like cording and lymphedema from taking hold, something many women with breast cancer often suffer from.

Physically I had a reasonably good level of fitness and so could continue with my normal exercise routines most of the time. However, if you are not fit and receive a cancer diagnosis, it's probably not the time to commit to a strenuous fitness program. You will need to ease in with gentle exercise and walking.

When my treatments started, my husband took off more days than usual to help out, but he also wanted to use this precious time together to go out and create memories. Some of these adventures, however, were more successful than others.

Bicycling was something my husband and I enjoyed doing together. Once a month we would try to have a date day, and this would more times than not see us pedalling away to some destination or another, when he organized our dates. I suppose it was his Dutch blood that gave him his love of cycling! I shared this love, as I discovered it to be a most beautiful way to take in the creation around you, instead of whizzing by it in a car and missing so much of its beauty.

One memorable outing happened after my second chemo treatment. The plan was a forty-kilometer loop. My husband thought that would be all I could handle in my condition. About halfway through the return trip, I asked him if he could get the car and pick me up. He replied by assuring me we were almost there (famous last words which I had heard many times before on many such adventures!). Well, I couldn't pedal one more rotation, and promptly let my bike fall on the front lawn of an old age home we happened to be cycling past and I proceeded to lay down in a heap. My body would no longer listen to my mind. It had reached its limit.

Another cycling trip occurred after my fourth chemo treatment. I was quite unwell by then, but my brother and his wife were over from Canada and I desperately wanted to show them Rottnest Island, a beautiful holiday destination about an hour off the coast of Western Australia. There was only one problem—this island had no cars and we would have to ride bikes everywhere! When we arrived, we picked up our rental bikes and began cycling. I wondered why they would rent me a bike that had such flat tires. I complained to my husband, and, after he checked, he assured me that my tires were fine. It wasn't my tires. It was my body, exhausted from chemo, which made it feel like I was cycling on tires that were flat. But I refused to quit. I kept going.

Another unforgettable occasion was participating in the five-kilometer Australia Day fun run a few weeks after my first chemo treatment. Australia Day also happens to be my birthday, making this event even more special for me. The morning of the run dawned beautifully. With an Australian flag wrapped around my bald head, I completed the run along with my husband, most of our children, and a neighbor. It was exhilarating to cross the finish line, even though I certainly didn't break any personal bests.

Exercising my body felt so good; it was like I could actually contribute toward negating the effects of cancer. It also gave a much-needed sense of normalcy during a time when so little else was normal. Not only was it good for my body, it was also beneficial for my soul. God created my body and soul to operate together, to complement one another, and it was important to recognize this vital connection and to work with it. God's children are redeemed, both body and soul, from sin and death, and one day—in eternity—our bodies and souls will be completely and perfectly restored.

I recovered from most of my many operations quite well, due, in part I believe, to diet and exercise. But over time, even diet and exercise couldn't stop the toll operations and treatments began to take.

There was one operation in particular I found hard to bounce back from, and I will never forget the night I came home from hospital. It was quite late, and I thought the children would all be in bed. But when we returned home, there they were, all six of them, standing in the garage waiting to welcome their Mama home. They were ready. Except they weren't. The expressions on their faces said it all: "You look terrible. You don't look like our Mom." That day made me all the more determined to keep my body in as best fighting shape as I could, to keep things as normal as I could, for my sake and for the sake of those I loved.

Body Image

Body image is a delicate subject to write about because in some ways I am quite a private person. But yet, to help others going through cancer, especially breast cancer, I feel I must touch on it.

Quite frankly, I struggled. I struggled with seeing my body, once created as a work of art by my Creator, being subjected to deforming attacks. It was akin to the devil marring God's perfect creation. Rebellious cancer cells were trying to destroy the body God had created beautiful. I knew that beauty is what's in your heart, but I suppose I was surprised at how much of my identity also seemed to be anchored to my outward appearance.

I struggled with seeing my body, once created as a work of art by my Creator, being subjected to deforming attacks.

I found it deeply confronting and disturbing that breast cancer and its treatments attacked everything about me that was feminine. Even my long, dark hair was gone! My fingernails and toenails couldn't be painted because they were weak, loose, and split. Scars were appearing everywhere, which troubled me deeply. Infections often set in, making matters worse. It got to the point where I asked my husband to take down all the mirrors in our home. I simply couldn't bear to look at myself.

The body I had tried so hard to take care of was in ruins. It seemed that not only my soul needed restoration, but my body now needed it too. And in time, in God's time, I was blessed that it did receive restoration. As I write these words I can feel my hair resting on the back of my neck and am thrilled that I need shampoo once again. I can look in any mirror and be happy and go to any beach and not be self-conscious.

No, I wasn't as I once was, however I am overjoyed at the restoration I have received this side of eternity and know that my perfect restoration of body is still to come.

Body and Soul

As I beheld the work God was doing to my soul, I knew that He would give me everything I needed for my body as well. After all, I was not my own, but belonged with both body and soul to my faithful Savior.[29]

My body had been subjected to much physical pain—sometimes a little, sometimes a lot, sometimes manageable, sometimes not. Measuring pain on a scale of "one to ten" became a relative exercise.

My body had also been subjected to loss and deformation. This deterioration was due to the fall into sin. It made me realize that my body was perishable; it wouldn't last forever. But it would eventually be sown and—one day—raised as imperishable (1 Corinthians 15:42).

But part of me still wondered: Why these vessels that so easily crack and break? Could it be that the very curse that caused the body to be subjected to decay, causing these fracture lines, had been reversed by God to allow His glory to be displayed through the very cracks of brokenness? Is God so great a God that He turns the darkness of sin into good? Does darkness show us worlds of light that we don't see by day?[30]

These are incomprehensible things, things that I can only stand in awe and wonder of. They are things Paul preached about. He wrote: "For God, who said, 'Let light shine out of darkness,' made His light shine in our hearts to give us the light of the knowledge of God's glory displayed in the face of Christ" (2 Corinthians 4:6). Although subjected to the fall into sin, the body remains the

[29] *Heidelberg Catechism*, Lord's Day 1.

[30] Moore, *The Comforter.*

temple of the Holy Spirit and is intrinsically connected to the soul. And so, somehow, my body and soul—both of which belonged to my faithful Savior—were shining the light of God's glory.

How amazing.

My body had been put through so much adversity, but now my night of ruin was slowing turning into my morn of song. I was sure that the day would come when I would be able to read the quote my daughter printed out for me without tears blurring my focus: "Scars remind us that, though we were wounded, we've been healed."[31]

I had been bought at a great price—the blood of my Savior. His Spirit resided in me and therefore I was to honor Him with my body—a body that was restored in part now and would be restored fully in eternity.

---

31 Lee, *A Moment to Breathe*, 96.

Twelve

The Spiritual Provision

My ears had heard of You but now my eyes have seen You.

JOB 42:5

How do you begin to describe the Provision Who is indescribable? Who can grasp the extent of His purpose and plan? Job confessed God's sovereign Kingship when he said: "I know that You can do all things; no purpose of Yours can be thwarted" (Job 42:2). And so, our most important provision, our greatest gift, is purely God's presence in our lives.

Our relationship with God permeates all of life, and knows no borders. It intertwines everything, connecting body, mind, and soul. It's inseparable from any part of our lives, because our lives are hidden in His Son, Jesus Christ, the Immanuel—God with us. And so, God's spiritual provision is always there, always near, and always in our hearts.

If all we had was the provision of God with us, would He be enough? The answer is a resounding "yes" for all who bear His name, for all who share in His anointing. The amazing grace of being grafted into Christ and having His Spirit in our hearts is all we will ever need.

This grace, however, is not a grace that stops there. Its power reaches even further. God, in His great love for us, gives His children grace upon grace (John 1:16 ESV). Through this grace we receive so many other provisions through The Provision of Himself. We've looked at some of them already: gifts of relational love, mental capacity, emotional stability, and physical endurance. These are all conduits employed in dispensing God's grace. They are conduits we are responsible for tapping into as we press on.

Let's delve into some of the spiritual graces God employs in allowing us to experience His Presence in our lives.

The Bible

What a treasure trove the Bible is! Over the years I have spent much time in this timeless Book. I know its words, read it regularly, and feed my soul diligently. But something changed once I began travelling cancer's road.

The Bible graduated to becoming my survival manual; it became a book I treasured above all others, a book I began taking with me wherever I went, and it showed. Particularly, the pages of Psalms and Isaiah displayed signs of frequent use. I was realizing anew how amazing the words of the Word really were! I had read the Bible since childhood, but now it was different, somehow. I no longer viewed it as a generic conversation God had with His people, but rather, I now saw it as a conversation He was having with *me*—a personal letter written from God to His daughter, a daughter who was navigating her way through the brokenness of life and desperately needed the comfort and assurance of her Father.

The stability of God's Word began to strike me more and more. I knew the Bible's truth was timeless and never changed, even though the world did. But I had never really valued that attribute like I did now, when everything else around me seemed to be in a constant state of flux.

Another attribute that struck me was the potentiality of the Word of God. This refers to how the Holy Spirit endows its readers with the very aspect required for their particular time and circumstance. This amazed me! I uncovered new applications in the same verses I had read all my life and saw new things in the same verses I had read countless times.

What a dynamic, powerful, resilient, timeless, indestructible, and unchanging book of truths God's Word is! What a nourishing and life-giving source of comfort and hope, what a portrayal of our God its pages contain. What a provision for my journey. I ate it and it tasted as sweet as honey (Ezekiel 3:3) and left me wanting more. God's Word was my lifeline, connecting me to Him. I became desperate to know Scripture better, to know God better.

Firstfruits

Being able to take God's Word with me into every minute of my day became possible only through the spiritual discipline of dedicating the firstfruits of my time to God. I had, for the most part, always conversed with God on a daily basis, but it would usually happen when it fitted into my schedule. Devotion time would be something in my day that I allowed myself to put off, telling myself I would get to it eventually.

This all changed. The Bible now became the first thing I reached for each and every morning. Even feeling its pages as I turned them gave me comfort. It became the only way to start my day; the only way to shine light on my day. After my early morning devotion time, I tried to memorize one text or one portion from that day's reading to take with me. Over time, I became aware of the ease in which Scriptures came to mind just when and where I needed them, whether it was while driving to the hospital, sitting in the waiting room of my doctor's office, or during my scans.

I had to know that God was near, and the Word was my constant reminder that He was. John 6:35 captures our need poignantly: "Then Jesus declared, 'I am the bread of life. Whoever comes to Me will never go hungry, and whoever believes in Me will never be thirsty.'"

I had to know that God was near, and the Word was my constant reminder that He was.

It's a hard trek through the desert of suffering. If you need to make changes in order to feed your soul with the provision of God's Word, now is a great time to make them. Your very survival depends on it! You can't take a step forward without His Word being your compass. You will be lost without it.

Sundays

Worship

Going to church to hear the preaching of the Word of God, to partake in worship along with my brothers and sisters in Christ, now became not just an activity I simply enjoyed and knew I needed, but something that was essential to my spiritual endurance.

As a result, I attended church as often as I could, despite my medical limitations. There were Sundays where I attended church wearing a big jacket to hide all my drains, there were Sundays where I wondered what I would do if I became ill. There were Sundays where I wouldn't make it through without crying. But rarely was there a Sunday I stayed home. I couldn't stay away. I needed to hear God speak through His Word, I needed to sing His praises, and I needed to be with the rest of His body. I needed to be with Him in His house.

Day of Rest

I had always observed Sunday as a day of rest. I was taught this from a very young age, and knew it was a biblical ordinance. It was to be a day devoted to spending quality time with God, and so, a day where I didn't work; a day where, as a mother, I tried to create a special atmosphere in the home. But now, with the craziness of cancer, I appreciated Sundays as a rest day even more. I saw its beauty in the way it restored my body and soul in increased measure. Maybe it was waking up to the sounds of those well-loved hymns of old sung by the men's choirs, with their deep, resonant voices. Maybe it was the peace that Sunday brings, maybe it was the anticipation of going to church and hearing God speak, maybe it was the opportunity to worship God with His body of believers. Whatever it was, Sunday was a wonderful way to start my week, regardless of what that week held in store.

Prayer

"Prayer is the natural outgushing of a soul in communion with Jesus,"[32] wrote the great preacher, Charles Spurgeon. How true. Time spent *in* the Word becomes time spent *with* the Word Who became flesh (John 1:14). God speaks, we respond. It's the way of covenantal relationship.

When self-reliance and self-dependence are threatened, and you realize that you are completely reliant and dependent on God, you find yourself talking to Him a lot more. How amazing, really, that the Creator and Sustainer of everything and everyone wants to hear from us, sinful mortals. Moses realized how special a privilege this communion in prayer was, and made sure that God's people understood it too: "What other nation is so great as to have their gods near them the way the LORD our God is near us whenever we pray to Him?" (Deuteronomy 4:7).

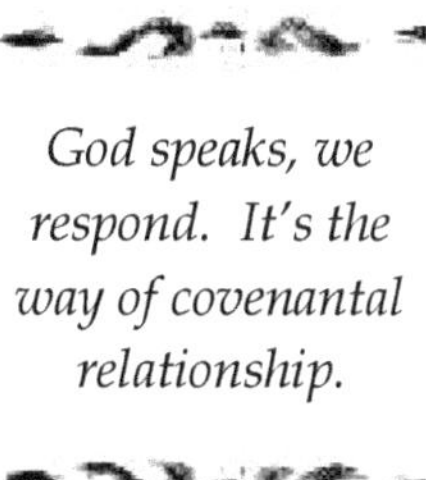

There's much to be written about prayer, too much for the pages of this book, so what follows is a summary of the provision it was

[32] Spurgeon, "The Secret of Power in Prayer," Metropolitan Tabernacle Pulpit, Volume 34.

for me through my days of affliction. For a more comprehensive look at prayer, I highly recommend the book, *Call Upon Me*.[33]

Prayer – A Covenantal Dialogue

God made a covenant with me to be my Father through Jesus Christ. He came to me first and sealed His promises at my baptism, and then as an adult I responded to His love and grace by committing my life to Him.

A vital part of this covenantal relationship was time spent with my Father in conversation. When I pray, I remind myself of God's place and mine in this most special relationship of love—God comes first, God speaks first, and then I respond. And so, I try to begin my prayers by acknowledging who God is and giving Him the praise He is due, before asking for things and letting God know about my weals and woes.

I realized the importance of this especially from studying the book of Job. The end chapters, particularly chapters 38–41, show us Who God is and who we are by comparison, putting us humans in our proper place:

> Where were you when I laid the earth's foundation? Tell me, if you understand. Who marked off its dimensions? Surely you know! Who stretched a measuring line across it? On what were its footings set, or who laid its cornerstone—while the morning stars sang together and all the angels shouted for joy? (Job 38:4–7).

It is only right to give God adoration for who He is before praying about anything else. He is worthy, no matter what may be going on in our lives. He is LORD, He is in control, He is in charge, and we can trust His will in our lives. Adoration of God and acknowledging Who He is reminds me of who I am: fallen, wretched, and undeserving. And yet, God wants to hear from me. That makes me overwhelmingly thankful. When I realize I

---

[33] Westerink, *Call Upon Me*.

deserved nothing but had everything because of God's grace, I see so many other things to thank Him for too.

Finally, then, and only then, with the right framework in place, do I unleash my petitions that, if not for the help of the Spirit, would be unleashed first, and not last.

This prayer sequence is sometimes known by the acronym of ACTS:

A Adoration;
C Confession;
T Thankfulness;
S Supplication.

Do you think using a pattern makes prayer a little too contrived? Too ordered? Lacking spontaneity? Can't we just pray anywhere, anytime? Of course we can! I sent up what I call "arrow prayers" frequently, especially in moments where I felt broadsided or out of control.

But picture yourself, for a moment, as a prayer warrior wearing a quiver on your back. When you spend time with God in relationship with Him, spending time really getting to know Him and enjoying intimacy with Him, you're busy putting arrows into that quiver. Then, when you need an arrow in the heat of battle, you draw one out, because there are plenty there! You have a relationship with God that you can draw on at any time. But if all you ever do is fire off arrow prayers, one day you may reach in your quiver and find nothing there. You have been neglecting your relationship with the One Who matters, and your quiver is empty.

Nehemiah was a Jewish exile, a cupbearer to the King of Persia, and his prayer life as recounted in the Bible book bearing his name demonstrates this quiver principle. The first chapter records for us his prayer conversation with God, a quiver-filling prayer if you ever did see one. Then, in chapter 2:4–5, Nehemiah finds himself in a quandary. The King asks him a question and demands an immediate answer, an answer that will have far-reaching implications. With no time to sit down and commune with God extensively, what does Nehemiah do? He reaches for an arrow from his well-stocked quiver, sends it up to God, and proceeds to answer the King.

If we want a meaningful relationship with God, we need to make it a spiritual discipline to spend time with Him every day. To carve out time from our busy days. To treat our relationship with God as our most important relationship and invest time and vulnerability into it. When Someone means everything to you, and you can't survive a day without Him, it won't prove difficult.

There were days, however, when I reached into my quiver much more often than I was busy filling it up, days when I struggled to even remember a proper prayer framework. There were days when I found it hard to be thankful for anything and, quite simply, didn't have the energy to adore God. There were days when I would go directly to petitions, petitions that came thick and fast. There were days when I was too tired to look at my sins, much less confess them. These were days when I called on the Holy Spirit to intercede for me (Romans 8:26–27), days when I relied heavily on others' intercessory prayers.

Yet overall, I strove for balanced and meaningful dialogue with God first thing each and every morning. I found if I maintained the correct sequencing in my prayers, things were placed in their proper perspective and my gaze of Who God was and what He was doing was widened—widened from my small circle of existence to His all-encompassing plan for His Church, for the world, and ultimately, for His glory.

I was humbled that, in the middle of this incredible sovereign plan of God that was conceived before the foundation of the world, there was room for me (Isaiah 46:10; 2 Timothy 1:9). I saw with increasing clarity how this sovereignty of God is a wise sovereignty, never making mistakes. Not only that, but overshadowing every single wisely-crafted decision God made for my life was His perfect love, meaning His sovereignty was never indifferent or uncaring. I felt more and more peace realizing that God's sovereignty meant that His plans for me were good.

Prayer as a Weapon

Prayer is a powerful weapon in the battle of good versus evil. In this battle, we are told to put on the full armor of God and so be strong in the Lord (Ephesians 6:10–11). Realizing that our struggle is none other than against the spiritual forces of evil, we must pray in the Spirit on all occasions (Ephesians 6:12, 18).

Armed with the Word and prayer, we can withstand the attacks of the evil one. And attack he will. God may use pain as a megaphone, but Satan also uses our pain, however with deception and lies thrown in the mix. Just as God's presence is intensified in suffering, Satan also uses this time to discover chinks in the Christian's armor, and to up the ante in his fight for your soul.

It's hard to think about, and, to be honest, difficult to write about, but it's important to realize who our enemy is, what he's capable of, and what he's not capable of. We dare not underestimate or overestimate his powers.

When I pause to consider Satan's attacks, I get emotional. And so, tears stain these very pages. Tears of sadness, about how unrelenting the devil's attacks are toward those who belong to God, tears of sadness in how our old nature loves to help the devil in this. Tears of joy, about how faithfully God carries His own. Tears of joy seeing how God progresses our new nature in Christ. Sadness and joy, both intertwined. Darkness and Light. Brokenness and Beauty. Both there.

Despite the mortal wound inflicted on Satan when Jesus defeated death on the cross and rose again, assuring the outcome of good over evil, the battle rages on. It will continue to do so until the time of complete restoration, the time of the End, when Jesus returns to close the circle opened in Paradise and ushers in the dawn of a new age.

Until then, we live in a broken world. Life on the battlefield isn't easy, but the provision of prayer is invaluable. I like to imagine that prayers from the battlefield are carried directly to God's throne by special angels as a provision for those who are in the fiercest of fighting. Prayers for God to remember His promises that He will be with us and will never forsake us. Prayers for perseverance, endurance, faithfulness, and strength. Prayers for Him to remind us always that nothing can separate us from His love in Christ Jesus.

Indeed, nothing can separate us from the Provision of Himself and His love. As Ann Voskamp writes: "When His Love's got a hold of you there isn't a lie in the universe that can pull you apart."[34] Romans 8:38–39 is biblical proof of her words: "For I am convinced that neither death nor life, neither angels nor demons, neither the present nor the future, nor any powers, neither height nor depth, nor anything else in all creation, will be able to separate us from the love of God that is in Christ Jesus our Lord."

Realize that Satan wants your soul and will use devious means in your time of suffering to try to make you question God and His goodness.

Realize that Satan wants your soul and will use devious means in your time of suffering to try to make you question God and His goodness. He'll try to make you collapse in times of emotional weakness, try to make you give up when you are physically exhausted, and try to make you shake your fist at God in the face of bad news. He'll try to attack your marriage, your relationships. He'll enlist your old nature in trying to make you fall.

Satan is waiting to tempt you in your testing. Resist him with the Word and prayer. Flee from him and run to the shelter of the Most

---

34 Voskamp, "Dear Little Lies that are keeping us up late."

High. Nothing can separate you from God's love when you are safely under His wings.

Pray Continually

Prayer helps prepare and sustain you for whatever your day ahead may hold. The day before radiation began, I was meditating on 1 Thessalonians 5:17 where Paul instructs us to "pray continually." My accompanying devotion reminded me that the awareness of our constant need for reliance on God, which some would interpret as a weakness, was actually our greatest strength. Praying continually keeps us mindful of this need and reminds us that our strength isn't what gets us through, but rather our dependence on God's power (2 Corinthians 12:9).

And so, our emptiness is filled with hope—not in our ability to cope, but in God's ability to sustain. Then our inadequacies no longer lead us to despair but to dependency; our emptiness is not filled with problems, but with His presence.

And we need God's presence every moment of our lives, or, as the old hymn goes: "I need Thee ev'ry hour, most gracious Lord. No tender voice like Thine can peace afford."[35] Praying continually, creating thought patterns where we lift our eyes to God, seeking His face, and finding refuge in Him, sustains us and provides balm for our hurting and tired souls.

Prayer and God's Sovereignty

When someone finds themselves in particularly difficult circumstances, such as a serious illness, it becomes increasingly important for them to understand the biblical place of petitioning in prayer. Perhaps it's because there's so much at stake that we wonder whether prayer can alter our circumstances, whether prayers do, indeed, change outcomes. This is one of the reasons why we are often drawn to the Psalms during times of affliction—

[35] Annie Hawks, "I Need Thee Ev'ry Hour."

we, too, join their chorus of crying out to God and pleading with Him to answer our prayers.

But the quandary with prayer and petition happens when God's answers don't seem to align with what we think He should answer—that His plans for our good aren't necessarily what we would consider to be good. We struggle, when God's will doesn't align with our will.

Is it perhaps because we think we are in a better place to determine how the story of our life should unfold? That we want a say in which events should happen and which events shouldn't, as if, somehow, we know better than God what to do in our lives?

If we want to write our own story, then we are guilty of the sin that's been there from the beginning: the sin of pride. The sin of thinking we know better than God. The sin of enthroning ourselves, and dethroning Him.

If we want to write our own story, then we are guilty of the sin that's been there from the beginning.

Really, we want God to do what we want Him to do. And so, before petitioning God in prayer, it becomes crucial to examine our motives and subject them to His will. Is it our heart's sincere desire to bring God glory, no matter what that means to our circumstances? Is our response as trusting as the response of Daniel's three friends who were about to be thrown into the furnace?

> If we are thrown into the blazing furnace, the God we serve is able to deliver us from it, and He will deliver us from Your Majesty's hand. But *even if* He does not, we want you to know, Your Majesty, that we will not serve your gods or worship the image of gold you have set up (Daniel 3:17–18, emphasis mine).

Do you believe that God is working for your good and His glory *even if* He chooses not to answer your prayers for healing, but rather delivers you by taking you to your eternal Home? Of course, we should not become fatalistic Christians and just think

God is going to do what He's going to do and there's nothing we can do about it. No. That's not a relationship! Daniel's three friends wanted God to deliver them and knew He was able, but still subjected their will to His. The persistent widow (whose story is found in Luke 18) certainly wasn't going to take "no" lying down, continually entreating God until He answered. The Psalms, too, are full of pleading for God to hear His people and answer.

God desires us to ask things of Him, but with the right motivation and the willingness to subject ourselves to His answer. James 4:2–3 reads: "You do not have because you do not ask God. When you ask, you do not receive, because you ask with wrong motives." Humility should be our prayer posture and God's glory the motivation when we petition God. We must never demand that God listens to our voice rather than us listening to His. He is the Potter, we are the clay (Isaiah 64:8).

Does Prayer Change Things?

That still leaves us with the question: Does petitioning God change actual outcomes? Let's turn to the Bible for answers.

Several examples can be found in the Scriptures. One compelling example is the story of King Hezekiah told in 2 Kings 20:1–11. In this passage, we find King Hezekiah terminally ill. Isaiah, the prophet, came to visit him. "Put your house in order," he told the King. "You are going to die; you will not recover." But does King Hezekiah roll over and just wait to die? No! Instead he "turned his face to the wall and prayed to the LORD, 'Remember, LORD, how I have walked before you faithfully and with wholehearted devotion and have done what is good in your eyes.'" Then we are told that Hezekiah wept bitterly. What happens next? Isaiah wasn't even off the palace grounds before God told him to turn around and tell Hezekiah that his prayer had been answered. His life would be extended for another fifteen years! Prayer changed things.

Another powerful example is when God's anger was aroused because Israel had made a golden calf and was worshipping it.

God said to Moses: "I have seen this people, and they are a stiff-necked people indeed! Let me alone, so that I may destroy them and blot out their name from under heaven" (Deuteronomy 9:13–14). What does Moses do? He falls prostrate before the LORD, fasting for forty days and forty nights, eating no bread and drinking no water. He intercedes before the LORD on behalf of the people (as a type of pre-figuring Christ). What happens? The LORD listens to Moses and spares Israel from complete annihilation. Prayer changed things.

But the most instructive and moving scriptural example comes from God's own Son, Jesus, and His agonizing prayer in the garden of Gethsemane before His crucifixion: "'Father, if you are willing, take this cup from Me; yet not My will, but Yours be done.' An angel from heaven appeared to Him and strengthened Him. And being in anguish, He prayed more earnestly, and His sweat was like drops of blood falling to the ground" (Luke 22:42–44).

Jesus knew He had to die. There was no other Son of God to take His place. He was the One and Only. He knew the cup couldn't pass. Yet He asked for it to. God's answer came in the form of a provision—an angel was sent to strengthen Jesus. Because of both God's justice in punishing our sin, and His mercy toward sinners, Jesus' prayer didn't change things, couldn't change things.

Even though God has foreordained everything from before the foundation of the world, never think that this negates your prayers and petitions. Even though we can't comprehend this dichotomy, one doesn't exclude the other. Don't become a fatalistic Christian.

God's Word shows us that He has a hidden will and a revealed will (Deuteronomy 29:29). His revealed will is found in His Word. His hidden will has not been revealed to us. Does that mean we can't pray about things that exist in God's hidden will? No, it most certainly doesn't! Because in some mysterious, unexplainable, amazing, wonderful, and humbling way, God uses our prayers in the formation of His secret will.

How is that possible if that will is preordained? We don't know. The Bible doesn't answer that for us. But we don't really need to know. What we do need to know is God's revealed will about prayer as found in James 5:16: "The prayer of a righteous person is powerful and effective."

Does God change what's written on the pages of your life if you plead before Him, if your church pleads before Him, if your family, your friends pray unceasingly? Let's leave that up to Him. But know that He will hear every last prayer through Jesus Christ. He will answer and it will impact on His will in a way we cannot, as humans, ever understand. God operates outside of time as we know it, in a dimension we can't even comprehend. So no, we don't understand the link between our petitions and God's preordained will. But we don't have to. It's not our place to fathom His counsel. It's our place to trust it.

God is sovereign over all. He has perfect reasons why He answers our prayers the way He does. Look back on your life and recall His deeds, His faithfulness to you. Be confident that what He is busy doing for you now is perfect! Rest in the knowledge that He knows what's best and wants to give you that best:

> Which of you, if your son asks for bread, will give him a stone? Or if he asks for a fish, will give him a snake? If you, then, though you are evil, know how to give good gifts to your children, how much more will your Father in heaven give good gifts to those who ask Him! (Matthew 7:9–11).

Armed with this knowledge, bring your requests before God. He is writing the story of your life. He has all your days, your pages, numbered. He will safely bring you to your eternal Home.

So, does prayer change things? It certainly changes us, changes our perspective, and yes, it sometimes changes our circumstances. God answers our prayers by giving us an understanding of Who

He is, that what He does is loving and wise toward us. Armed with this awareness, we begin to realize that everything that is going on in our lives is happening within the bounds of God's eternal plan. Not a hair will fall from our heads without His will. And that's rich comfort for any cancer sufferer.

Prayer changes us, changes our perspective, and sometimes changes our circumstances.

Prayer and Reasoning

The Bible gives some instances of righteous saints reasoning with God in prayer. One such example can be found in Genesis 18:16–32, where we see Abraham pleading with God for the city of Sodom. Another instance is when God Himself says to His people Israel in the midst of their unfaithfulness: "Come now, and let us reason together" (Isaiah 1:18 NKJV).

Having learned that God's sovereignty and my prayers could co-exist, coupled with the knowledge that anything is possible with God, gave me confidence to reason with God in prayer, bearing in mind that I must do so humbly and with reverence for Who He is.

My reasoning went something like this: "Six times I stood at the baptism font with my husband and vowed that I would raise Your covenant children in the fear of Your name. I can't do that, God, if I'm not here. Please heal me."

I also reasoned on behalf of my children: "I will walk through this, LORD, but please, don't allow my children to grow bitter and turn from you as a result of this hardship, but rather make them better and stronger in their faith through this experience."

Prayer and Waiting

The Bible often uses the phrase: "When the time had fully come" before introducing a life-changing event. We, too, are called to "wait on God" when it comes to God answering prayer. Not only are God's ways not our ways, but His timing also isn't our timing.

God created humans to live in time and we can't go one second back or one second ahead. We can't control time.

Perhaps we unwittingly consign God to our time and space and look for His answers within these realms of our understanding. But God is the Alpha and Omega, the Beginning and the End, the One that is, was and is to come (Revelation 1:8). When His time has fully come, He will act, He will answer, and that answer will come in the perfect time and in the perfect way.

Prayer and Positive Thinking

Many things have been written about the importance of having a positive mindset during suffering, as if that's all that's needed. But is it? Is positive thinking enough to change outcomes? If I were to channel all my positive energy toward being cured, would it impact the results?

While being positive is a great mental and emotional stabilizer that God uses in our lives, it is no substitute for prayer. We have much to be positive about as God's children, but our positive thinking needs to be directed toward trusting God, not directed toward our own power to alter outcomes. Be positive, by all means, positive that God has hope-filled plans for you, just as He did for His people in captivity:

> 'For I know the plans I have for you,' declares the LORD, 'plans to prosper you and not to harm you, plans to give you hope and a future. Then you will call on Me and come and pray to Me, and I will listen to you. You will seek Me and find Me when you seek Me with all your heart'(Jeremiah 29:11–13).

Prayer for Others

Praying friends, relatives, or fellow church members is an amazing provision. Some of my most heartening moments have been when I would meet someone (sometimes even someone I barely knew) and they would say: "Oh, you're the woman with cancer. It's so nice to meet you as I've been praying for you a lot." How humbling! How loving!

The body of Christ was bringing me before God's throne. They hurt when I hurt. Their prayers not only comforted me, but God used them to strengthen me. See this as an urgent call to prayer. God uses the prayers of others as a vehicle for strengthening and extending love to those in need. The sufferer will be carried by them and will feel the peace of Christ rest upon them.

Prayer – Summarizing Thoughts

How astounding it is that the God of the universe wants to hear from me, a sinner! It's almost as if God pities us because we perceive His plans for our lives so dimly and so feel the need to posit our limited viewpoints to Him. As if we could tell the Maker of heaven and earth, the Master of all humankind, what He should do in any given situation! And yet, that's what He wants—not for us to tell Him, but to ask Him, while acknowledging all the while that His will for our lives is perfect, and so praying for His will to be done. In this way, we go forward in hope and dependence, trusting that God, in His time, in His way, will make us all beautiful in our broken.

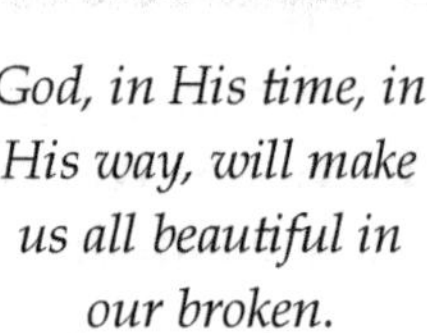

Intimacy with God

When you seek God with dedication, listening to Him speak through His Word and responding to Him in prayer, something amazing happens in your relationship: you experience intimacy. Your relationship flourishes. Abiding in Him, being connected to Him, results in receiving continual nourishment as we travel from our temporal existence toward our eternal one.

Experiencing the intimacy of this connection in a most tangible way during suffering is a spiritual provision beyond compare. It's true, you can experience intimacy with God during good times. You can have intimacy with God in your everyday normal routines. But we seem so much more aware of it during the difficult, dark days. Could it be that our struggles push us to God, push us to spend time with Him and His Word, and that as a result, intimacy increases? That our intimacy increases as our knowledge of, exposure to, and time spent with God increases?

When something like cancer rears its head, we need God to be tangible in our intangible situation, and become driven, as a result. Driven to the Word, driven to our knees in prayer, driven to the throne room of God. We experience Him in ways we perhaps never did before. This intimacy is an enormous provision for the sufferer; it's almost like receiving a foretaste of what perfect intimacy in eternity will be like.

They say every cloud has its silver lining. If the cloud is refining, the silver lining, shining more brightly and more luminous than anything imaginable, is the intimacy God gives to those in the refining fires. How big the cloud is, how dark the cloud is, how ominous the cloud is, no longer matters. All that really matters are the silver lining and the end result—the salvation of our souls (1 Peter 1:9). As Elisabeth Elliot once penned: "The deepest things that I have learned in my own life have come from the deepest suffering. And out of the deepest waters and the hottest fires have come the deepest things that I know about God."[36]

Job also experienced a deep intimacy with God. Job 1:1 tells us that Job was a blameless and upright man, fearing God and shunning evil. You would think Job experienced an intimate relationship with God that could not have been improved upon. And, yet, when we get to the last chapter of Job, what do we discover? That through all the afflictions Job endured, through all his refining, his relationship with God had changed—vastly. Job describes the change like this: "My ears had heard of You but now my eyes have seen You" (Job 42:5).

I knew God before I had cancer. I believed in Him. I worshipped Him. I loved Him. I served Him. But now I see Him and His glory much more clearly. What a treasure.

[36] Elliot, *Suffering is Never for Nothing*, 9.

Puritan Willem Teellinck wrote these compelling words: "Though days of affliction are sad, dark, and unwelcome, they nevertheless will become the most fruitful days of your life."[37]

We, too, are learning Who God is, and who we are, through our afflictions. We are learning that being pruned results in bearing fruit that lasts, fruit that gives God the glory. Teellinck calls them "fruits of tribulation"[38] and promises that "The cup of suffering, which God mixes for their good, will never be stronger than the godly are able to take."[39] The seeds of affliction God sows in our lives will yield a great harvest. There is no easier way.

Your journey through your desert will give you beauty in the brokenness of your affliction. Open your ears and hear God speak. Open your eyes and behold His glory. The provision is there: the gift of Immanuel, God's Presence with you.

"Now the LORD blessed the latter days of Job more than his beginning" (Job 42:12 NKJV). Job knew, more than ever, the God he loved and served. Job's refining resulted in a relationship with God he didn't know was possible. May the same be true for you.

---

[37] Teellinck, *The Path of True Godliness*, 122.

[38] Teellinck, *The Path of True Godliness*, 114.

[39] Teellinck, *The Path of True Godliness*, 115.

Psalm 91

1 Whoever dwells in the shelter of the Most High
will rest in the shadow of the Almighty.
2 I will say of the LORD, "He is my refuge and my fortress,
my God, in whom I trust."

3 Surely He will save you
from the fowler's snare
and from the deadly pestilence.
4 He will cover you with His feathers,
and under His wings you will find refuge;
His faithfulness will be your shield and rampart.
5 You will not fear the terror of night,
nor the arrow that flies by day,
6 nor the pestilence that stalks in the darkness,
nor the plague that destroys at midday.
7 A thousand may fall at your side,
ten thousand at your right hand,
but it will not come near you.
8 You will only observe with your eyes
and see the punishment of the wicked.

9 If you say, "The LORD is my refuge,"
and you make the Most High your dwelling,
10 no harm will overtake you,
no disaster will come near your tent.
11 For He will command His angels concerning you
to guard you in all your ways;
12 they will lift you up in their hands,
so that you will not strike your foot against a stone.
13 You will tread on the lion and the cobra;
you will trample the great lion and the serpent.

14 "Because he loves Me," says the LORD, "I will rescue him;
I will protect him, for he acknowledges My name.
15 He will call on Me, and I will answer him;
I will be with him in trouble,
I will deliver him and honor him.
16 With long life I will satisfy him
and show him My salvation."

PART THREE:

THE DESTINATION

Then we shall see face to face.

1 CORINTHIANS 13:12

I had done a lot of travelling and come a long way. But the journey wasn't quite finished yet. I had glimpsed the final destination, tasted it, and its hope propelled me onward. I knew its beauty awaited me. And, when confronted with the brokenness of this present world—in myself, in others, and in creation—it made me long to be there now.

I had prayed so often, so fervently, that I could have more time on earth before I arrived at my eternal destination, time to fulfill my vows made before God: vows to commit my whole life to the LORD's service, vows of being a help-meet to my husband, vows of raising my children in the fear of God's name.

What a quandary. I was thankful I wasn't the One Who made the call as to how long it would be before I entered my eternity. Only Someone perfect in wisdom, perfect in love, could ever make that decision perfectly. What was it Paul had once said to the Philippians? "For to me, to live is Christ and to die is gain" (Philippians 1:21).

And so, I pressed onward to my destination with God preparing me, refining me, helping me to re-enter day-to-day living. I pressed onward, seeing Him working in others at the same time as me, preparing us all for our eventual arrivals: the day we will see His glory face-to-Face.

May you, too, continue to travel onward till that great and glorious day. The day when we will see clearly why God takes the path He does with us. The day we will know fully, experience fully, His glory and His love, a love that never fails.

A love that abides forever.

Thirteen

The Preparation

There is a time for everything,
and a season for every activity under the heavens.

ECCLESIASTES 3:1

When you're about to take a journey, you need to prepare. Looking back, God prepared me for my journey through cancer by giving me provisions to store up in readiness. I didn't realize it at the time—but in retrospect, I see that He did.

I had received a solid upbringing, having been taught the Scriptures from when I was young. I had had God's promises sealed on my forehead at baptism. I was raised to walk in newness of life before God, being told that my rebirth into a spiritual creature was made possible by Christ's death on the cross in payment for my sin.

I enjoyed spending time with God, in relationship with Him. I diligently studied the Scriptures and knew that Hebrews 12:6 said: "The Lord disciplines the one He loves, and He chastens everyone He accepts as His son."

I knew that meant me. One day. I just didn't know when or how. In fact, in the few months before my first diagnosis, I did a Bible study on Psalm 73. If meditating on these verses of the Bible doesn't prepare you for refining, nothing will. I felt Asaph's confession of God's presence and protection were words I could now take on my own lips and claim for my own life:

> Yet I am always with You; You hold me by my right hand. You guide me with Your counsel, and afterward You will take me into glory. Whom have I in heaven but You? And earth has nothing I desire besides You. My flesh and my heart may fail, but God is the strength of my heart and my portion forever (Psalm 73:23–26).

My cancer diagnosis placed me firmly on the launching pad, on the verge of a spiritual growth spurt, so to speak. God was building on the foundation that had been laid, and showing me it was time to live out of the promises I had known and believed for so long.

Following Jesus

The road that Jesus walked was one of suffering, pain, humiliation, and abandonment. My suffering could never be compared to His, yet our journey shared this: they required obedience and trust and would lead to spiritual rewards. I knew that God would be with me, leading me, guiding me, but that did not remove the necessity for me to pick up my cross and follow Him.

Up until now, following Him had never been terribly hard. Oh, there had been moments of trial and tribulation in my life, to be sure, but this was different. This was so "up close and personal." I was learning that the real cost of following Jesus was walking through suffering before arriving in glory (2 Corinthians 4:17). This is the road Jesus walked. This is the road I needed to walk. I suppose I thought that glory might come without intense suffering. I thought wrong.

It was daunting but, in a way, exciting! Things that I had read about on the pages of God's Word, things God had promised would happen in the lives of His children in order to produce a harvest of righteousness, were now happening on the very pages of my life (Hebrews 4:4–12).

Living in a Fallen World

Living in a fallen world has consequences for body and soul, and so, both body and soul need to be restored through Christ. I knew deep down that instead of asking *"why me?"* after my cancer diagnosis, the real question perhaps was *"why not me?"* After all, sin is responsible for brokenness entering the world; for alienating us from God. We all stand guilty. Romans 3:23 makes that clear: "For all have sinned and fall short of the glory of God."

I knew deep down that instead of asking "why me?" the real question perhaps was "why not me?"

But God, in His great mercy, came up with a plan for healing and reconciliation, for restoration, through His only Son Jesus Christ. This obedient Son submitted to His Father's will, leaving His glory behind to pay for our sins and reopen the way back to intimacy with the Father. Jesus Christ is The Way Home, The Way to our Destination. Isaiah 43:6–7 reads: "Bring my sons from afar and my daughters from the ends of the earth—everyone who is called by My name, *whom I created for My glory,* whom I formed and made" (emphasis mine).

On this road to glory we don't walk alone and we don't walk without purpose. Our days here are but a preparation ground for our eternity of days. And so, we live each day in hope, even as God prepares us by refining us through times of suffering. But our hope is not one just reserved for the future. God's Kingdom begins here and now with its fulfillment awaiting! Armed with the hope of God's love for you, of God's plan for you, of the future God has in store for you, you are prepared and readied. Ready to be refined and grow in His image. Ready to be a vessel displaying His glory, a glory that is displayed in the midst of and in spite of your very brokenness.

Don't be anxious because the time of refining, of uncovering, of growth has come. Embrace it in trust. And realize it happens in God's perfect way, in God's perfect time, to all those the Father loves (Hebrews 12:5–8). I'm sure if you look back on your life, you can see God preparing you for such a time as this. Just like He prepared me, just like He prepared my cousins, just like He prepares all His children for what He has planned for them.

Biblical Examples of Preparation

God will prepare us for what lies ahead. But we need to make use of the means He gives for this preparation.

By the time David was called in from the fields and anointed, his foundation was firmly in place. He had been prepared.

Think of David as a shepherd boy. All those peaceful, lovely days beside still waters, tending his father's sheep, composing psalms surrounded by green pastures. David was being prepared for the times to come. No, David didn't realize then that he would be spending years living on the run from King Saul, nor that he would one day become a warrior king. He certainly would not have known that he would be instrumental in the birth of the Savior of the world. But David used the preparation time God gave him to develop his relationship with and knowledge of God. By the time David was called in from the fields and anointed by Samuel, his foundation was firmly in place. He had been prepared for what was waiting for him.

The Bible provides more examples, too. God prepared Noah for the flood by giving him many years to build the ark. Moses' years in Pharaoh's court and with his father-in-law as a sheep-herder in the desert gave him ample preparation for the great task to lead the people of Israel out of Egypt into the desert en route to the

Promised Land. God prepared Nehemiah to return with the exiles from captivity and rebuild Jerusalem's walls, by giving Nehemiah the position of cup-bearer to the king. God has tasks for each one of us, tasks that often take us through times of suffering and affliction in order to accomplish them.

Going Forward in Faith

If your foundation is in place, then when it's time to traverse the deep valley, you are equipped, you are trained, yes, you are even ready to traverse it with God at your side.

God will not lead you to something that He won't lead you through. He walks beside you. He strengthens and encourages you. His grace always provides a way. When Esther was faced with having to risk her life to prevent the slaughter of her Jewish people, her cousin Mordecai came and said to her: "And who knows but that you have come to your royal position for such a time as this?" (Esther 4:14).

God doesn't do anything randomly. He has a purpose for your suffering, a purpose that leads to His glory and your good. Just as Esther had her moment, we all have our moments. Moments which we know that God has been busy preparing us to meet. What unites all these moments is that they are growth moments, moments we will all be confronted with at some time or another—because God prunes those He loves. Pruning produces a harvest of growth. So, don't shrink away from your suffering, or it will produce nothing but bitterness, and your branches will produce no fruit. Rather, trust that God, in His loving and wise sovereignty, has ordained this for your life at this time.

J.C. Ryle reflected on how we can have rest in our afflictions:

> Let us seek to have an abiding sense of God's hand in all that befalls us, if we profess to be believers in Jesus Christ. Let us strive to realize that a Father's hand is measuring out our daily portion, and that our steps are ordered by Him. We should try to feel in the day of trial and disappointment, that all is right

> and all is well done. We should say to ourselves, "God could keep away from me these things if He thought fit. But He does not do so, and therefore they must be for my advantage. I will lie still, and bear them patiently."[40]

God is at work in your life! Rest in Him, trust in Him, and be faithful. You may not always feel prepared for what you are going through, but know that He will sustain you through it, and give you what you need as you need it. The suffering you are now enduring, will, also in time, prove to be a means of preparedness of its own: a preparedness for your eternity with God.

God is sanctifying you, making you grow in love for Him and others "so that you may be able to discern what is best and may be pure and blameless for the day of Christ, filled with the fruit of righteousness that comes through Jesus Christ—to the glory and praise of God" (Philippians 1:10–11).

You will face difficult stretches on your journey. We're not in the rich oasis of the garden of Eden, but in the desert of suffering with the devil as a roaring lion, wanting to devour us. Don't be surprised at your fiery ordeal as though something strange were happening to you, 1 Peter 4:12–13 tells us. Instead, rejoice, seeing your sufferings as participating in Christ's sufferings, and prepare to be overjoyed when Christ's glory is revealed.

Suffering will only last a little while. Some of us will be healed during our lifetimes. Others of us will be healed through death and entrance into eternity. There is, after all, a time to be born and a time to die.

We are told to travel, and, by the grace of God, that's exactly what we'll do. And when we reach our goal, and the Chief Shepherd appears? We will receive our crowns of glory that will never fade away. So humble yourself under God's mighty hand, cast your anxieties on Him, resist the devil, stand firm in the faith, and then know this: "And the God of all grace, who called you to His

---

[40] Ryle, *Expository Thoughts on Luke: Volume 2*, 61–62.

eternal glory in Christ, after you have suffered a little while, will Himself restore you and make you strong, firm and steadfast" (1 Peter 5:10).

"Strengthen your feeble arms and weak knees" (Hebrews 12:12). It's time to go through the valley en route to your destination, fellow-pilgrim. You've been prepared. You've been readied. Step forth in faith.

There is a time for everything. And your time is now.

Fourteen

The Suffering

The Lord gives you the bread of adversity and the water of affliction. Whether you turn to the right or to the left, your ears will hear a voice behind you, saying, "This is the way; walk in it."

ISAIAH 30:20–21

There is nothing glamorous about suffering. It's tough. Brutal. Painful. Challenging. Frustrating. Ruthless. Not only is your own body being attacked, but throughout all your operations and treatments you come into contact with many other people suffering as well. Some will live, some will die.

Suffering takes many forms. Our minds naturally construe it to be primarily physical. But it's so much more. We've already seen that suffering also contains relational, mental, emotional, physical, and spiritual elements. Although everyone's suffering will be impacted by each of these factors, our relational adeptness, our mental capabilities, our emotional fortitude, our physical condition, and our spiritual foundation will all play a role in determining which areas we suffer in the most.

My journey of suffering seemed to be a journey of continual loss—step by step, operation by operation, treatment by treatment. At times I wondered when and where things would end and if I could endure. I didn't know why God used suffering as a means to accomplish His purposes with me, but I did know it was effective. John Piper writes:

> No one ever said that they learned their deepest lessons of life, or had their sweetest encounters with God, on the sunny days. People go deep with God when the drought comes. That is the way God designed it. Christ aims to be magnified in life most clearly by the way we experience Him in our losses.[41]

Suffering and Glory

We can experience peace in the midst of extreme suffering by understanding that our pain has a purpose. God has a reason for everything He does and will accomplish what He has set out to accomplish. What does He aspire to bring about with our suffering?

His Glory!

We need to aspire to this same goal. After all, that is the chief purpose of our existence, to glorify God. But what exactly does this mean? How do we glorify God in our sufferings? First, we should attempt to define "glory." It's somewhat difficult to do this. Merriam-Webster provides this explanation: "Worshipful praise, honor, and thanksgiving."[42] John Piper writes that God's glory is "the infinite beauty and greatness of God's manifold perfections."[43] God is perfect in all His attributes, and envelops holiness and glory. It is Who and what He is. We, as His children, need to recognize, acknowledge, and live for His glory in everything we say, do, and go through.

Paths to Glory

One way suffering brings about God's glory is that it grows our obedience. Even Jesus, Hebrews 5:7–8 tells us, learned obedience

---

[41] Piper, *Don't Waste Your Life, 73.*

[42] *Merriam-Webster Dictionary,* s.v. "glory."

[43] Piper, "What Is God's Glory?"

through what He suffered: "During the days of Jesus' life on earth, He offered up prayers and petitions with fervent cries and tears to the One who could save Him from death, and He was heard because of His reverent submission. Son though He was, He learned obedience from what He suffered." We do the same; our obedience is being tested by suffering, and when our obedience matures through these tests, God is glorified.

Another way suffering leads to glory is that it enables us to become vessels, albeit broken ones, that hold, display, and share in Christ's glory:

> For God, who said, "Let light shine out of darkness," made His light shine in our hearts to give us the light of the knowledge of God's glory displayed in the face of Christ. But we have this treasure in jars of clay to show that this all-surpassing power is from God and not from us (2 Corinthians 4:6–7).

What a treasure the children of God have been given! God's glory is to shine forth from us, weak, brittle, cracked jars of clay. In our weakness we display God's strength, God's glory, in our lives. This is how God is pleased to use us. But God doesn't stop at allowing us to reflect His glory, but He also allows us, sinners, to share in His glory. How amazing: "Now if we are children, then we are heirs—heirs of God and co-heirs with Christ, if indeed we *share* in His sufferings in order that we may also *share* in His glory" (Romans 8:17, emphasis mine).

Understanding that suffering leads to glory doesn't mean we should glorify suffering in and of itself. Suffering shows us that this world is irrevocably broken and must be redeemed. Suffering reminds us of the fall into sin and its consequences. Suffering is not an end in itself but a prelude to a new beginning.

When we truly come to grips with what God is accomplishing through our suffering, whether we survive cancer or not seems somewhat superfluous. The only thing that matters is how we have displayed God's glory through either of those outcomes.

What matters is that what we've done, we've done for the glory of God (1 Corinthians 10:31).

No Shortcuts to Glory

Human nature wants to gloss over the suffering part of life, and just get to the glory part. But there are no shortcuts to glory; no shortcuts for us, no shortcuts for Jesus Christ. Think of Satan's defeat: we wish we could gloss over the war between God and Satan and fast-track to the victorious part—Satan's eternal demise and consignment to hell and Jesus returning for His Bride. And it's good that we fix our eyes on this goal! But it's necessary to pause and ponder the cost of this victory over evil, the suffering that it involved and continues to involve.

Human nature wants to gloss over the suffering part of life, and just get to the glory part.

The gift is in the contrast. The beauty restored is only beautiful because it emerged from the broken. The glory is made more glorious because of the suffering that preceded it, much as mercy is so much more merciful because of the justice our sins deserve. God's light shines greatest in the darkness.

Satan had already brought about the demise of God's crown of creation by enticing mankind to rebellion, resulting in the fall of the human race and the creation being subjected to a curse. The cost of restoration was high—God's only begotten Son. And this One and Only Son suffered, in obedience to His Father and in love for you and for me. He suffered, for God's glory, only to receive back His own: "I have brought You glory on earth by finishing the work You gave Me to do. And now, Father, glorify Me in Your presence with the glory I had with You before the world began" (John 17:4–5).

Cancer is suffering, and suffering is hard. There is no shortcut, no way around it. There's only a Way through it. The question is not how you *feel* about suffering, but the real question is: how will you *use* your suffering? Will you use it to feed a bitter root toward

God? To behave as though the fall into sin was His fault? Will you shake your fist at Him in anger? Or, will you seek to glorify God with your willing obedience and unshakeable trust in His plans for your life, seeking to glorify Him in and through your suffering?

When Jesus began His journey to the cross, He had His eyes fixed constantly, resolutely, on the goal. He knew there was no shortcut, no easier way. Even though His soul was troubled, Jesus stayed true to the course, knowing it was for this very reason that He had come to earth (John 12:27).

Lazarus and Glory

Our goal must be to live our lives for God's glory, not for our comfort and ease. We learn this when we read about Jesus' friend Lazarus being sick (John 11:1–44). Lazarus' sisters, Mary and Martha, send for the Healer, Jesus. Surprisingly though, Jesus does not drop everything and come at once to heal Lazarus. No, instead He says: "This sickness will not end in death. No, it is for God's glory so that God's Son may be glorified through it." Then, two days later, He leaves for Bethany, the home of Lazarus, Mary, and Martha, telling His disciples that Lazarus had fallen asleep and that He was going there to wake him up.

God received more glory through Lazarus dying and being raised, than if He had simply rushed to Bethany to heal Lazarus. However, this meant much more suffering for those who loved Lazarus, and possibly even more suffering for Lazarus himself. But only in this way could Jesus' power over death be displayed, only in this way could resurrection life be shown. And so, events unfolded the way they had to unfold for God to receive the glory.

Jesus also suffered when Lazarus died—He even wept. Suffering isn't always easy for us—we may weep too. But take heart. Listen to Jesus' words to Martha: "Did I not tell you that if you believe, you will see the glory of God?" (John 11:40).

If our sole purpose of existence is to glorify God and enjoy Him forever, can we—shall we—lay everything down, open our fingers from their clenched fists, relinquish our cries of why, our pleas for deliverance, our hopes for an easy life, to a God who we know is working all things for our good and His glory? We must be willing to let go of our sense of entitlement to temporal blessings and see where the blessing truly lies: beholding God's glory, giving Him glory, and sharing in His glory.

Are you suffering? It has purpose, even when you have no idea where things will end up. Suffering has resurrection purpose and is hope-infused. Like Martha, believe! Believe that in your suffering you will see the glory of God. After all, isn't the goal of your life to be a glory-seeker?

Treasure and Glory

If the goal of our life is to seek God's glory at any cost, then we can begin to understand the parable of the kingdom-seeking, glory-seeking merchant looking for fine pearls. When he found one of great price, he sold everything he had to buy it (Matthew 13:45–46). Everything.

John Owen wrote this about the Parable of the Pearl of Great Price:

> The glory of Christ is the 'pearl of great price' which we should make every effort to find. And the Scripture is the ocean into which we dive to discover this pearl. Every sacred truth that reveals something of the glory of Christ to our souls, is a pearl or precious stone which enriches us. But when the believer discovers this pearl of great price itself, then his soul cleaves to it with joy.[44]

Discovering Christ's glory is finding a treasure beyond compare. If our suffering gives us glimpses into its incalculable value, suffering becomes more than worth it.

---

[44] Owen, *The Glory of Christ*, 33.

We may feel overwhelmed when we realize what a treasure we possess. But do you know that God views us as His treasure too? We are His treasured possession (Deuteronomy 26:18). We are all treasures in His treasured Kingdom because we share in His glory. His glory is the pearl of great price that we have become a part of through Christ's blood.

Did you know that a pearl is formed when a foreign object (usually a parasite) works its way inside the oyster? This bothers the oyster and causes it to release a fluid to coat the irritant, creating a unique, exquisite pearl. Well, Christ's blood coated us, coated our irritant sinful nature, creating us into a unique treasure for God in His Kingdom. Into exquisite treasure that displays His glory, that displays His work of creating beauty out of the brokenness—even the brokenness of sin.

This is a process that takes time. The journey can't be rushed, just like the formation of a pearl can't be rushed. But the day will come when the transformation is complete, when our brokenness is turned to beauty. Already now, you can see it: a foretaste. Our rebirth has happened; our restoration begun. We have become glory-seekers. Glory-reflectors. And by the grace of God, He won't stop and we won't stop until He completes in us what He started (Philippians 1:6) and we are welcomed into His Kingdom of Glory.

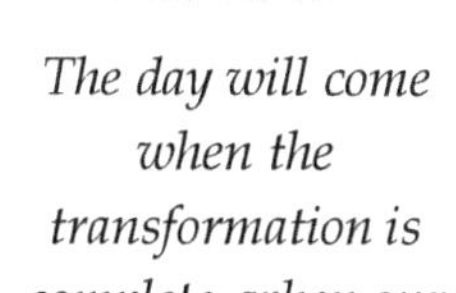

The day will come when the transformation is complete, when our brokenness is turned to beauty.

In the meantime, we press on, knowing that this phase of suffering is only temporary and will lead to glory unimaginable. Paul puts it in perspective for us: "For our light and momentary troubles are achieving for us an eternal glory that far outweighs them all" (2 Corinthians 4:17).

Suffering on one side of the scale, and glory on the other. There's no contest, is there? The weight of glory is unsurpassed.

Suffering and Scriptural Emphasis

At times, suffering is so difficult that we feel like our world is collapsing around us and we despair of life itself. We may even find ourselves questioning God's goodness and presence.

Paul D. Wolfe, in his book, *My God is True!*,[45] warns that in such times it is vital to apply proper spiritual punctuation. We shouldn't put question marks where exclamation marks go, or vice versa.

For example, we may be inclined to say:

> Is God even here beside me in my sorrow?

We turn a biblical statement into a question, since God's Word says that He will never leave us or forsake us (Deuteronomy 31:6). We should say:

> God is with me in my sorrow!

Other times we put in an exclamation mark when we should put in a question mark:

> There is unconfessed sin in my life and this is why things are happening to me!

Instead, James 5:15 tells us to consider the possibility of unconfessed sin. However, it doesn't say that there *must* be unconfessed sin. We should be asking and not exclaiming:

> Is there unconfessed sin in my life?

Paul Wolfe warns: "When Christians start listening for whispers from God that go beyond the Bible, the stage is set for profound disappointment and discouragement."[46] During times of suffering we need to exclaim the promises of Scripture and not question them.

Well-meaning people said different things to me about why I had cancer. One said: "God would never give you cancer—it's from

---

[45] Wolfe, *My God is True!*, Chapter 3.

[46] Wolfe, *My God is True!*, 41.

Satan." Another said: "Cancer is just a result of the fall into sin; God has nothing to do with it, but because He loves you, He will turn it to your good." Yet another asked: "Do you think God has placed cancer on your path?"

All these comments perhaps contain some truths, but lack the proper overarching scriptural emphasis. It certainly was not comforting, much less scriptural, to think that God had nothing to do with what I was going through! The Bible tells us that God has everything to do with everything: "Let the heavens rejoice, let the earth be glad; let them say among the nations, 'The LORD reigns!'" (1 Chronicles 16:31).

Charles Spurgeon, a preacher who suffered at the hands of debilitating depression, was always careful to use scriptural emphasis as a frame around his circumstances:

> As far as personal sorrows are concerned, it would be a very sharp and trying experience to me to think that I have an affliction which God never sent me—that the bitter cup was never filled by His hands, that my trials were never measured out by Him, nor sent to me by His arrangement of their weight and quantity. May we see that our heavenly Father fills the cup with loving tenderness and holds it out, and says, "Drink, My child; bitter as it is, it is a love potion which is meant to do you permanent good."[47]

Scripture emphasizes that suffering occurs as a result of the fall into sin. Disease came into the world through sin, sin not authored by God but used by Him for His purposes. Scripture also emphasizes that before the foundation of the world, God in His sovereignty ordained who would have cancer and who would not. Most importantly, Scripture emphasizes that the LORD reigns . . . over everything and everyone.

---

[47] Spurgeon, "Woe and Weal," Sermon 3239.

Let's maintain the emphasis that Scripture gives and not misrepresent Scripture in order to make God and His plan make sense to us.

Suffering and Refining

In Bible times, silver and gold were refined by breaking up the rough ore containing the precious metals. Next, the refiner put this broken ore into a melting pot called the crucible. This crucible was in turn put into the furnace and heated to the exact temperature necessary for removing the unwanted impurities. These impurities, or dross, would then form on the surface and be removed. After that, the refiner would turn up the heat even more and place the crucible back into the furnace. This happened time and time again until there were no more impurities left. Different impurities would rise to the surface under different temperatures. The refiner would know how the process was progressing by how clear his reflection would shine on the surface of what was being purified. He wouldn't stop until he was satisfied.

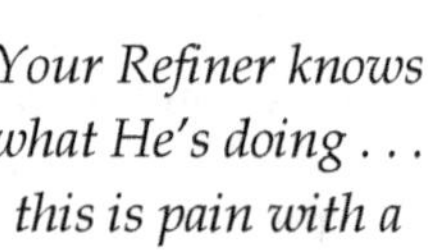

Your Refiner knows what He's doing . . . this is pain with a purpose.

Our suffering is purposeful pain. But pain it is, at times leaving you wondering how you will survive the intense heat. The temperature may be different for different pieces of ore, but for those who belong to God they may be sure of this: they will be refined in the exact way that is needed. The temperature for their refining will be perfect. The number of times dross is removed from them will be perfect. And that is because our Refiner is perfect. He knows you perfectly and so He makes no mistakes in your refining process. And the best part of it all? He will be right beside you the entire time, watching over you. You will be in His presence and under His constant care. And so, you will be able to say, along with Job: "When He has tested me, I will come forth as gold" (Job 23:10).

Your Refiner knows exactly what He's doing. He makes no mistakes. He's burning away your impurities. He's removing the haze, so He can see His image reflected in you. That's the Refiner's goal! God is taking your relationship with Him to a deeper level. Trust Him, and know: this is pain with a purpose. Satan will whisper his lies. After all, the battle for your soul is heating up. He doesn't want your impurities removed. And so, he will tell you that if God loves you He wouldn't put you in the fire. Don't believe a word of it. Believe the truth of the Word, instead—truth which tells us that God is refining us because we have been set apart to be His children, His image bearers.

Zechariah 13:9 speaks of God working to keep a remnant of people for Himself on this earth, a remnant set apart to be holy: "This third I will put into the fire; I will refine them like silver and test them like gold. They will call on My name and I will answer them; I will say, 'They are my people,' and they will say, 'The LORD is our God.'"

Refining accomplishes God's purposes for us to more and more reflect His glory in our lives. In this way we also grow in our state of preparedness, our state of holiness, for the eternal glory that awaits. We are the body of which Christ is the head, and so need to become holy, become mature, become changed into the image of Jesus Christ. As the Man clothed in linen explains to Daniel, refining is a very effective means of accomplishing this transformation: "Many will be purified, made spotless and refined" (Daniel 12:10).

Do you understand that God is refining you in order to change you? That God is sanctifying you, making you grow in righteousness? God's not going to *start* your refining on the day you enter eternity, He's going to *complete* it! Complete the good work in you that He has started (James 1:4). The Genevan Psalter's rhymed version of Psalm 138 puts this so beautifully:

> LORD, though I walk 'mid troubles sore,
> Thou wilt restore my faltering spirit;
> Though angry foes my soul alarm,
> Thy mighty arm will save and cheer it.
> Yea, Thou wilt finish perfectly

What Thou for me hast undertaken;
May not Thy works, in mercy wrought,
E'er come to nought, or be forsaken.[48]

Although our salvation attained by Christ's sacrifice on the cross is a salvation that's a completed gift of grace that we didn't and couldn't contribute anything toward, our growth in holiness is a work in progress; a work that is done for us, but never without us.

Growth in Christ occurs through many things, but seems to really blossom through adversity—through pruning—painful though it is. John 15:2 reads: "He cuts off every branch in Me that bears no fruit, while every branch that does bear fruit He prunes so that it will be even more fruitful."

Part of being in Christ means trusting Him and submitting to His Kingly authority, realizing that His pruning plans will accelerate your spiritual growth. In the process, we bear fruit that will last into eternity, fruit that brings God glory, and fruit that ensures we are ready to be harvested when Jesus Christ returns. It's fruit, Jesus says, that shows we are His disciples: "This is to My Father's glory, that you bear much fruit, showing yourselves to be My disciples" (John 15:8).

We may wonder why our spiritual growth is watered by the tears of suffering. We, too, like Job, often don't understand what God is doing in our refining. Job never knew that Satan came to God seeking permission to inflict suffering on Job. He just assumed everything he was receiving was from the hand of God. He knew nothing about the heavenly exchanges occurring, the battle of good versus evil being played out. We have the benefit of reading Job's entire story—we know it has a happy ending, both temporally and eternally. But Job didn't

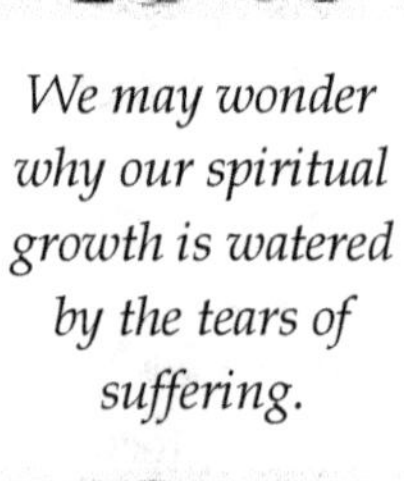

[48] *Anglo-Genevan Psalter,* Psalm 138:4.

know. He just clung to God in his suffering while accepting and trusting that God knew what He was doing, even though Job couldn't see or understand that purpose. Job 13:15 records Job's response: "Though He slay me, yet will I hope in Him." These words are words of faith and trust. The only terrible alternative is to take the words of death and distrust on our lips, the words spoken by Job's wife to her husband: "Curse God and die!" (Job 2:9).

Can you take Job's words of faith and trust on your lips? Do you desire to make what is important to God become important to you? Pray for growth in holiness, pray for God to refine you, remove your impurities, and so make you ready for meeting Him face-to-Face. If God decides to use suffering to expedite the refining process, accept that from His hand. The result will be worth it, because you will be presented to God as holy and blameless (Ephesians 5:27).

God is using events and circumstances to refine us, so that we glorify Him more and more. This process is not without pain. The refining is not without heat. But you will emerge beautiful. Beautiful in His eyes. Beautiful to those around you as you radiate His glory and love to a broken world. And that's the beauty found in suffering.

Suffering Well

When someone goes through an extended period of hardship, it can be difficult to continually maintain a biblical attitude toward suffering. I often think of how hard it must have been for the Israelites—forty years in the desert with the Promised Land at their very doorstep. Really, it isn't much different for us. We know that eternity awaits, and is ever so close, but we also know we have further to travel before we reach our Promised Land. Lifting and widening our gaze encourages us to see the bigger picture of our journey, giving us a glimpse of our destination. This keeps our suffering in perspective.

Jesus showed His followers how to suffer well. He knew the Scriptures and He communed regularly with God, often withdrawing to lonely places to pray (Luke 5:16). All this readied Jesus for His ultimate suffering: the road to the cross, a road He resolutely set out upon (Luke 9:51). Jesus knew the path ahead would contain unbearable suffering. His prayer in the garden of Gethsemane was agonizing: "Father, if You are willing, take this cup from Me" (Luke 22:42). Knowing His Father would turn His face away from His Son when He bore the sins of the world was almost too much for Jesus to bear. But because He did bear it, we will never have to suffer that same agony of being abandoned by God. Jesus did not resignedly accept the cross and His suffering. He embraced it. He suffered well, and asks us to follow Him in our suffering.

Besides our Great Example, we can also look to others who demonstrate to us godly ways of walking the road of suffering. Our family, friends, and the church community all provide us with examples of fellow-believers suffering in one form or another as a result of living in a broken world.

Search out the people that demonstrate scriptural truths in the way they suffer. Look to them as role models. Talk with them, learn from them, and be encouraged by them. No one has an easy life. It's impossible in a world that lies under the curse. But we do have redeemed lives, and our eyes of faith show us the way to suffer well, to suffer and endure like so many others, also those who have gone before. Follow their example.

Stay the course, fellow pilgrim, knowing and believing that you can travel this road in God's strength and with the encouragement of the saints. Seek God in every day you face, in every step you take, in every prayer you offer. Seek Him and you will find everything you need to walk on. As C.S. Lewis once wrote: "'Beloved,' said the Glorious One, 'unless thy desire had been for

Me thou wouldst not have sought so long and so truly. For all find what they truly seek.'"[49]

Do you feel like your pain will never end? Keep a proper perspective, an eternal perspective that enables you to suffer, and to suffer well. This life is not your eternity. It is your "little while" that will one day pass.

Dying Well

The Bible directs us to live in anticipation and expectation of meeting God face-to-Face at any given moment. This moment can happen when Jesus returns or when we die, whichever occurs first. Refining ensures we're ready for either prospect. We should all be seeing and living our lives in preparation for this Great Day, but so often we don't, instead getting side-tracked by the busyness of life and a myriad of seemingly important other things. A life-threatening disease forces us to stop and live like every day could be our last. Often it curtails our ability to do our other tasks, providing us with ample opportunity to reflect on important matters, such as mortality. This can be frightening for us and others around us, especially if we haven't thought about such things before, but it must not be delayed or ignored.

Death should not be a taboo subject. While we shouldn't be obsessed with it (as God numbers our days, not us) we do need to face up to its reality. I'll always remember the day my husband and I talked about the possibility of my death and what that would entail for our family. It was a most difficult and painful conversation, but beautiful, all in the same breath.

I am so thankful for the example Caroline was to me in her life, but, even more so, in her death. She showed that in Christ, it is possible to die well. In the end, she was longing for her better country:

---

[49] Lewis, *The Last Battle*, 56.

> All these people were still living by faith when they died. They did not receive the things promised; they only saw them and welcomed them from a distance, admitting that they were foreigners and strangers on earth. People who say such things show that they are looking for a country of their own. If they had been thinking of the country they had left, they would have had opportunity to return. Instead, they were longing for a better country—a heavenly one. Therefore God is not ashamed to be called their God, for He has prepared a city for them (Hebrews 11:13–16).

I had dealt with death before, but when Caroline died, I saw God preparing her and enabling her to do this well. I also witnessed people's different reactions to her preparation. Caroline struggled with others' unwillingness to accept her impending death, even though she herself knew she was approaching the closing chapter of her temporal life.

It raises an interesting and important question: If you have a terminal disease, at what point do you—or your family and friends—stop praying for a miracle of healing and accept that God's answer is, perhaps, "no" instead? If you never reach this juncture, will you have time to prepare for dying well?

At what point do you stop praying for healing and accept that God's answer is, perhaps, "no?"

In the cancer world, Stage IV means there's no cure (at present). You will, eventually, succumb to the disease, some much sooner than others, depending on the aggressiveness and spread of the cancer, the body's reaction to various treatments, and, most importantly, depending on the number of days God has allotted. Some Stage IV patients die in a month, while others live for quite some years.

Maybe the prayer for a miracle in this situation comes from knowing that, originally, we weren't created to die. Death came into the world through sin. But sin has come, and there is no denying that all of us will, one day, die, unless Jesus returns first.

Ecclesiastes 7:2 reads: "It is better to go to a house of mourning than to go to a house of feasting, for death is the destiny of everyone; the living should take this to heart."

For a Christian, death is not something to fear. True, we were born to live and should employ the means and blessings we have been given to that end. But healing shouldn't so completely absorb us that we fail to think about or look forward to what is in store for us on the other side of the Jordan. If we anticipate Who and what awaits us there, we can have peace with a Stage IV diagnosis. And if we have peace, those around us can and should strive to have peace with it as well.

It is hard for someone facing death to be told by others to be more positive in their thinking, as if there is something wrong with accepting God's answer to prayer as being anything different from earthly healing. I'm not saying a miracle isn't possible—it certainly is, and miracles do happen! But praying for a miracle in the face of end-stage cancer is like praying for someone who is in a wheelchair to walk again, or for the blind to see.

Can God do it? Absolutely. However, there comes a time when we need to accept that God is answering our prayer in a different way than we had asked for. Sometimes, He gives us that answer through test results, doctors' conclusions, and strength and acceptance of our situation, enabling us to die well. If others, then, continue to tell the terminally ill, "Don't give up, keep praying for healing," is that really helping them? Or is it denying them encouragement and comfort at a time when they need it the most, implying that death would be the worst possible outcome?

Again, I remember something Caroline said: "The worst that could happen to me is that I could die and be with the LORD. Would that be so bad?" Indeed, would it? Paul D. Wolfe, in *My God is True!*, writes:

> The reign of God over our lives should never lead to passivity. There was a good fight to be fought but we did so knowing that the outcome of that fight—whether the thrill of victory or the

> agony of defeat—was in the Lord's hands. We also knew that even if I lost the cancer-fight our heavenly Father would use that defeat to bring about the most thrilling victory of all: my entrance into the presence of my Savior.[50]

If we truly believe the hope we have in Jesus Christ, then we can do what Paul Wolfe instructs the sufferer to do: "Stop presuming you are going to survive this illness, as if God had guaranteed it, and start rejoicing in the thought of what awaits you even if you do *not* survive it. Set your hope firmly there, in heaven, where Christ is, where your citizenship is too!"[51]

In order to encourage one another to die well, we need to become more comfortable with death. We must learn to number our temporal days (Psalm 90:12) and, then, and, only then, can we live those days wisely, whether we are given great length of days or not. As Corrie ten Boom wrote: "Hold everything in your hands lightly, otherwise it hurts when God pries your fingers open."[52] Our days have been written in God's book before we were even born (Psalm 139:16). Death is not the end. It's only the beginning. "To live is Christ and to die is gain," Paul tells us (Philippians 1:21). Let's enjoy each day we receive, living for Christ, realizing that when God calls us Home, we gain even more. So many years ago, John Bunyan acknowledged this when he wrote:

> If, therefore, when thou hast fled, thou art taken, be not offended at God or man: not at God, for thou art His servant, thy life and thy all are His; not at man, for he is but God's rod, and is ordained, in this, to do thee good. Hast thou escaped? Laugh. Art thou taken? Laugh. I mean, be pleased which way soever things shall go, for that the scales are still in God's hand.[53]

God is sovereign. By being His child, His chosen and precious possession, God works out His sovereign plan in a perfectly wise and loving way. His wisdom means that He makes no mistakes

---

50 Wolfe, *My God is True!*, 25.

51 Wolfe, *My God is True!*, 44.

52 ten Boom, "Corrie ten Boom Quotes."

53 Bunyan, *The Works of John Bunyan, Volume 2*, 726.

with you and your circumstances. His love means that stretching above this wise sovereignty is His canopy of perfect love for His children, a love that is so powerful that it drives out fear (1 John 4:18). God has your best in mind—even if that best means limiting your time in the desert and bringing you across the Jordan sooner than you expected. Trust that your Father is sovereignly executing His wise plan for your life with unending love for you. "The LORD reigns, let the earth be glad" (Psalm 97:1).

Live well. But, if God is calling you Home, die well, knowing that for those who love God, the best is yet to come.

Suffering and Joyous Hope

Suffering well and dying well means that we display our hope and joy in Christ while traversing the desert plains of suffering en route to the Promised Land. It's a hope and joy not determined by our circumstances, or by our feelings, but by our outlook.

God has a blueprint for our journey; a blueprint to restore us as His image bearers. Paul lays this plan out for us in Romans 5:3–4: "We also glory in our sufferings, because we know that *suffering* produces *perseverance*; perseverance, *character*; and character, *hope*. And hope does not put us to shame, because God's love has been poured out into our hearts through the Holy Spirit, who has been given to us" (emphasis mine).

It's a hope and joy not determined by our circumstances, or by our feelings, but by our outlook.

James agrees with Paul, even exhorting us to consider suffering as pure joy: "Consider it pure joy, my brothers and sisters, whenever you face trials of many kinds, because you know that the testing of your faith produces perseverance. Let perseverance finish its work so that you may be mature and complete, not lacking anything" (James 1:2–4).

Do you see it? Our suffering leads to joyous hope—hope of restored glory. But this is not just something we anticipate, but something we can enjoy already now, in part. We can have hope and joy in the midst of our suffering, realizing what God is accomplishing through our pain. This sure conviction allowed Paul to reveal to the Philippians that he wants to share in Christ's suffering in order to gain, be found by, and know Christ (Philippians 3:8–10).

You may worry that suffering means you will lose joyous hope. Nothing is further from the truth. In fact, if you cling to God and turn to His Word, the opposite will occur. You will find that hope does not disappoint. You will discover joy in your suffering, knowing God is working toward the salvation of your soul. "I consider that our present sufferings are not worth comparing with the glory that will be revealed in us" (Romans 8:18).

Suffering? It's hard. But it's oh, so gloriously full of joyful hope.

Suffering and Gratitude

Checking our gratitude levels as we travel through our hard season is something that will go a long way to ensuring a bitter root does not grow in our hearts. What is your thankfulness gauge reading right now? Is it registering? Are you able to give thanks in all circumstances? (1 Thessalonians 5:18).

We don't need to thank God *for* everything that happens to us, but rather *in* everything that happens to us. When the results of the fall into sin strike, we can still be thankful. For what? For God's presence and for the good that He will accomplish through it.

With eyes of faith we can see that there is so much to be thankful for every day again. Is your heart still beating? Did you wake up this morning? Is the sun still shining, are the birds still singing? Are you a child of God? Is God with you, right here, right now? Does God have a plan with your suffering and will He use it for your good and His glory?

Suffer with gratitude for what you do have. Be thankful that God will never leave or forsake you (Joshua 1:5). He will even carry you if you can't walk. God is beside those He loves every step of the way, and that is why in all things we can give thanks. Ann Voskamp, in *The Way of Abundance,* writes: "Thanksgiving in all things accepts the deep mystery of God through everything."[54] God is the Creator and Sustainer. He is LORD over all, including us. We don't have a right to complain about the state of our lives. We're not in charge. God is. "I form the light and create darkness, I bring prosperity and create disaster; I, the LORD, do all these things. Woe to those who quarrel with their Maker, those who are nothing but potsherds among the potsherds on the ground. Does the clay say to the potter, 'What are you making?'"(Isaiah 45:7, 9).

Is your hand in God's hand or have you pulled your hand away, turning it into a fist instead?

It's not our place to question God. It's our place to give Him thanks, even amidst adverse circumstances. Job learned this the hard way, and makes this incredible confession of faith: "The LORD gave and the LORD has taken away; may the name of the LORD be praised" (Job 1:21).

Is your hand in God's hand, thanking Him for walking through suffering with you, or have you pulled your hand away, turning it into a fist to shake at Him in anger instead? The choice is yours to make. You *can* have a thankful heart toward God even when you do not *feel* thankful for the circumstances you are in. You can grieve, and still be thankful. You can hurt, and still be thankful. You can be angry at sin, and still be thankful. Giving thanks to God keeps our hearts in a right relationship with Him and saves us from a host of harmful emotions and attitudes that will rob us of the very peace God wants us to experience.

Understanding that illness is a consequence of the fall into sin also helps you to have a thankful heart instead of an angry heart. When God created the world perfect, there was no disease or breakdown

---

[54] Voskamp, *The Way of Abundance*, 158.

of the body. That only happened as a result of Adam and Eve's fall into sin. Things on this earth simply haven't been the same ever since. We now live East of Eden, and, as a result, sickness and suffering have entered our lives. That wasn't God's doing. It was ours.

If you fail to recognize this, and instead blame God for what you are going through, you cut off all chances of happiness and peace. C.S. Lewis put it this way: "God cannot give us a happiness and peace apart from Himself, because it is not there. There is no such thing."[55] Without God, we have nothing and no one to hold onto, no refuge from the storm. There is no peace apart from God. And so, practice the joyous discipline of a thankful heart and give thanks to God through good days and bad. Take these words of life and liberty found in Psalm 62:6 on your lips: "Truly He is my rock and my salvation; He is my fortress, I will not be shaken."

What should fill us with thankfulness the most is the priceless gift of God's only begotten Son, Jesus Christ. A gift given freely because God loves us and wants to restore the relationship that we damaged by sin. When we understand the depth of this love, we will delight in God, and will truly be able to give thanks always.

The moment will come when you will see that what God is doing in your life is for your good and His glory. Maybe you are already glimpsing this now. Can you recognize His work of transformation, as He encourages you onward to the day when you receive your crown and white robes in eternity? Can you see that He is slowly removing the veil that dims your gaze?

Kara Tippetts, in a remarkable witness of her faith, wrote on her blog shortly before her death: "What better way could I spend my last breaths than in thanksgiving?"[56]

---

[55] Lewis, *Mere Christianity*, 50.

[56] Tippetts, "Sacrifice of Thanksgiving."

Thanksgiving means giving praise to God for Who He is and what He's done for you in Jesus Christ. Thanksgiving means you don't blame God for having to navigate your life in a fallen world, but rather thank Him for helping you traverse its terrain. Thanksgiving means embracing the suffering before the glory.

Thanksgiving sees that the circle broken at the fall will be restored by the Restorer. Thanksgiving sees that we walk along this path of restoration in God's strength. Thanksgiving sees that suffering exposes the beauty that lies in glorifying God and looks forward to sharing in that glory.

Concluding Thoughts on Suffering

One day, the LORD will bind up your bruises and heal your wounds. It will be a day when the moon will shine like the sun (Isaiah 30:26). A day when you reach the end of your temporal story that God has written for you and find that the last line of Volume One reads: "And she lived happily ever after." A day when you reach for Volume Two, only to discover it's a Book with no end.

In the meantime, walk on, dear pilgrim. God is refining you by giving you the bread of adversity and the water of affliction. He is preparing you for your Homecoming. And, so, in your suffering, give thanks, and sing, and let your heart rejoice. Your destination is the mountain of the LORD. Follow Him there with a thankful and hope filled heart.

This is your Way. Walk in it. In His strength, you can.

Fifteen

The Re-entry

I am making a way in the wilderness
and streams in the wasteland.

ISAIAH 43:19

Is it possible for a Christian to grow so accustomed to being in the furnace of affliction that they find it difficult to re-enter everyday life?

Maybe I had become so used to the heat of refining, that when I re-entered the world, I felt awkward and extremely unprepared for what greeted me there. Everything seemed so different—so unrefined, so temporal, so tainted. I no longer saw or experienced things in the same way as I once had.

I needed to come to terms with no longer being in the "cocoon" of experiencing God's shelter and love in a most palpable way. It's almost like I had to be weaned off the extra provision of intimacy my Father had wrapped around me, to help me survive the high temperatures while in the furnace of affliction. All this left me feeling confused, unsure, and somewhat alone. It was like having to learn to walk all over again.

In the midst of this confusion, The Provider provided once more. This time, it was through a "chance" meeting with a lady that "happened" to be visiting our country church, someone I knew from when I had lived in the city many years ago. I hadn't seen her for a long time. We had started talking, and I sensed an instant spiritual camaraderie with her. As a result, I let myself become vulnerable, expressing how much I missed the intensity of relationship I experienced with God during my time of cancer, and how I was struggling to re-enter my "old life" once again.

This woman told me that her mother had gone through a similar experience. She had been carried so closely by the LORD in the time immediately following her husband's death, but then, about a year later, it seemed like the cotton wool of increased intimacy with her Father had slowly been unwrapped, and God had gently placed her back into her daily life. God was still there, but the cotton wool, the extra provision of a deep sense of His presence, was no longer required in the same measure.

After that conversation, I realized that the same was happening with me. Although God's presence would always stay with me, the cocooning under His wings where I had felt completely safe and at peace was a provision for the harshest legs of my desert march. God would remain with me on my entire journey to the Promised Land, but, no longer cocooned, I felt somewhat exposed. I had to relearn how to enjoy my relationship with God outside of this special covering. I had to find my feet *in* this world, while not being *of* this world (John 17:14–15), and this division post-cancer was a lot sharper than it had once appeared. His Presence would remain with me, but not always in such a tangible and remarkable way.

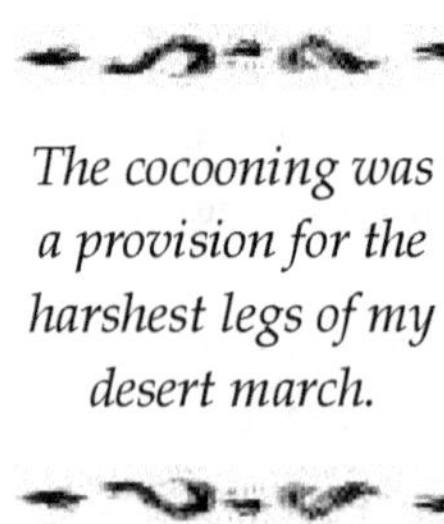

The cocooning was a provision for the harshest legs of my desert march.

I wondered if the High Priest had felt similar feelings after the Day of Atonement. How amazing it would have been on that one, special day a year to go behind the veil and enter the Holy of

Holies and experience God's Presence in such an overwhelming way. How difficult it would have been for him to leave again and re-enter his normal life.

As I had struggled to come to terms with being unwrapped from my cocoon, I discovered a passage that speaks about the greater glory of the New Covenant. I'm sure I had read these words many times, but never had it made such an impact on my heart:

> Now if the ministry that brought death, which was engraved in letters on stone, came with glory, so that the Israelites could not look steadily at the face of Moses because of its glory, transitory though it was, will not the ministry of the Spirit be even more glorious? For what was glorious has no glory now in comparison with the surpassing glory. Therefore, since we have such a hope, we are very bold. We are not like Moses, who would put a veil over his face to prevent the Israelites from seeing the end of what was passing away. But their minds were made dull, for to this day the same veil remains when the old covenant is read. It has not been removed because only in Christ is it taken away. Now the Lord is the Spirit, and where the Spirit of the Lord is, there is freedom. And we all, who with *unveiled faces contemplate the Lord's glory, are being transformed into His image with ever-increasing glory*, which comes from the Lord, who is the Spirit (2 Corinthians 3:7–8; 10; 12–18, emphasis mine).

Being out of the cocoon had made me feel like the glory had departed. But this passage showed me it hadn't. The glory hadn't disappeared, because God's Spirit hadn't disappeared. His transformation would continue as I was ushered into the next phase of transformation. I wasn't bereft. The Holy Spirit dwelt in my heart, in my broken vessel, and I would continue contemplating the Lord's glory, whether in the cocoon or not.

My re-entry was the path I needed to be on. I didn't have to be afraid, because I was following The Way. God had made a path through the mighty waters, and now was doing a new thing. I was travelling safely with Him, whether in the cocoon or out.

It was time to go forward, and not stay at the foot of the mountain. The glory wasn't going to stop; it was to be ever-increasing as I continued onward, doing the works God had prepared for me to do. It was time to step into my new normal, a new normal where I could recount all the wonderful things God had done for me; a normal that would ensure that the experience of God never became greater than God Himself; a normal that was thankful for the new creation I was becoming; a normal that sought to glorify God in everything.

Even though this period of transition had been difficult, I moved forward in confidence. Not in myself, but in God, who had proved to me time and again that all His promises are true. And, now, I had this blessed assurance going forward, that the same God who was there for me in the past would be there for me in the future, no matter what it held. Many uncertainties remained, but there was nothing uncertain about God and His promises; promises He had proved true on the very pages of my life story; promises that guaranteed that what He was doing in my life was good. What grace! Ann Voskamp writes: "Grace is what holds you when everything's breaking and falling apart, and whispers that everything is really falling together."[57] Indeed.

Although the umbilical cord to the cancer world had to be severed, my umbilical cord to Jesus Christ would never be severed. It would continue to pulsate with the life-giving blood only He could supply. God would be with me "to the very end of the age" (Matthew 28:20), and this included my time of re-entry back into a world where I still had a mission to complete.

I needed to hold on to this promise as I re-entered the world that seemed so foreign to me. I needed to hold on to this promise during my time of perceived loss of the deep provisions God provided. I needed to hold on to this promise when I struggled to relate to the day-to-day situations of normal life.

---

[57] Voskamp, *The Broken Way*, 192.

People tell me I'm different now—that I've changed. I'm hesitant to ask them what exactly they mean by that. In what way? Physically? Spiritually? Am I better than I was? Worse? I considered this in my quiet moments and in time I realized that yes, I had changed. The heat of refining had accomplished that change.

As I pondered all this, I thought once again to the words of Romans 8:28 and wondered if I was now ready to claim them for myself. Had God turned cancer to my good? The answer was . . . yes! Although cancer was not something I would ever ask for, it was something I no longer wanted to give back. It had been what I needed. Needed to change me for my good and—most importantly—needed for the increase of God's glory. If I had not changed as a result of all God's work, surely, I was to be pitied. But I had changed and I was humbly thankful for it. The Bible says that "God disciplines us for our good, in order that we may share in His holiness" (Hebrews 12:10). God was, and still is, busy refining me, changing me into the person He wants me to be. There's a word for that: *sanctification*! The next time someone said to me that I had changed, I would be sure to answer: *"I certainly hope so."*

Although cancer was not something I would ever ask for, it was something I no longer wanted to give back. It had been what I needed.

As I stepped out of the fire of my refining, into living my new normal, I still had bad days, days where I worried and was anxious, days where I felt I didn't belong. But I had something more: I had peace, living my life hidden in Christ, knowing that nothing could change that—especially not cancer.

The same God who enabled me will enable you—not only to walk through the mighty waters, but how to walk once you are on dry land. Never underestimate His promises, His love, and His power, no matter where you are at on your journey. You will only falter if you let go of Him or doubt Him. Go forward in faith and trust and leave the rest to Him. Go forward, always hidden in Him, looking to Him for strength, courage, and reassurance along The Way.

God has given each one of us seasons in our lives. Enjoy every single one. You've now got a new set of glasses on. Glasses that have sharpened your vision to perceive the temporal state of this life and the eternity that awaits; glasses that enable you to see normal everyday blessings as the special treasures they are. Glasses that enable you to see God's glory in a whole new Light.

God has made a way in the wilderness for you to travel and streams in the wasteland for your provision. You have been formed and made by God, created for His glory. So, walk on. Fulfill your purpose. Re-enter life, knowing God has summoned you by name and you are His—forever.

Sixteen

The Weaving

I will tell of all Your deeds.

PSALM 73:28

I loved it when I read it.

A friend had emailed me a poem entitled, *The Master Weaver*.[58] I had come across variations of it before, but it was so perfect for where I was at now.

To appreciate this poem, it's helpful to understand something about the weaving process. To make a canvas, the "warp threads" are held steady on a loom, as the "weft threads" cross over and under each warp, while the shuttle moves steadily from side to side. It's a complicated and time-consuming process, and great concentration is needed. At long last, the beautiful pattern, only hinted at along the way, fully emerges. All the effort is worth the

[58] The author of *The Master Weaver* is unknown.

resulting beauty, even though it was not always apparent why certain threads were used at certain times.

I had often wondered how the threads of my life would be woven together on God's loom into the canvas He had perfectly designed for me. Perhaps Joseph, so long ago, had wondered the same.[59]

Joseph was the second-youngest of twelve sons and was loved and favored by his father Jacob over his brothers. Jacob wove a coat of many colors for Joseph, inciting even more jealously from the others. One day, Jacob sent Joseph to check on his brothers who were grazing their father's flocks at least a day's journey away. Upon seeing Joseph from afar, the brothers' jealousy gave birth to a plan to kill him. Only the quick-thinking actions of the eldest, Reuben, stopped Joseph's blood from being spilled. Instead, the brothers stripped Joseph of his coat, threw him in a pit, and later sold him to passing by slave traders. Now they had to come up with a story that explained Joseph's absence to their father. So they took Joseph's coat of many colors, dipped it in the blood of a goat, and gave it to Jacob, along with their story that insinuated Joseph had been killed by a wild animal.

The threads of that terrible day were used in the pattern God was perfectly weaving in Joseph's life, and, ultimately, were used in the pattern of God's entire redemptive plan. Through a series of incredibly woven events, Joseph was given charge of not only Pharaoh's palace, but also of the entire land of Egypt. He was answerable only to Pharaoh himself (Genesis 41:39–40).

One of Joseph's duties became the distribution of food during a time of worldwide famine, a famine that saw Joseph's brothers coming to Egypt in search of grain. On their second such trip they encounter the most surprising and unbelievable turn of events: their brother is not only alive, but had been exalted from slave to Pharaoh's second-in-charge. The tables had been turned. Because

[59] Joseph's story can be found in Genesis 37–50.

of Joseph's high position, it was the brothers that needed to fear for their lives!

How does Joseph react to seeing his once-malicious brothers after some twenty-odd years? Not as you would expect. He wept loudly, and said: "Do not be distressed and do not be angry with yourselves for selling me here, because it was to save lives that God sent me ahead of you. So then, it was not you who sent me here, but God (Genesis 45:5, 8).

Joseph received Pharaoh's permission to move Jacob and his family to Goshen, the best part of Egypt, where they settled and increased. Upon Jacob's death, the brothers once again worried about Joseph possibly taking revenge. But over the years Joseph had seen the Master Weaver at work in his life in unfathomable ways. He had seen that the weaving of the most dire circumstances could be redeemed for good. And, so, he responds to his brothers' fear: "Do not be afraid, for am I in the place of God? But as for you, you *meant* evil against me; but God *meant* it for good, in order to bring about as it is this day, to save many people alive" (Genesis 50:19-20 NKJV, emphasis mine).

The Hebrew word used for "meant" is a verb that means "to weave."[60] God wove the dark threads of Joseph's life for good, creating a most glorious pattern. The dark threads had been redeemed by the blood—not of a goat—but of the Lamb! The brokenness of sin in the family of Jacob was being turned to beauty by the Master Weaver.

Seeing Joseph's canvas unfold on the pages of Scripture allows us to see why dark threads are so needful in our lives too. It hushes our questions of why, instead helping us to see that the Master Weaver makes no mistakes with His thread choices and is in total control of the loom. It enables us to trust Him for the perfect

[60] *Strong's Concordance,* s.v. "chashab."

pattern to emerge, a pattern we only see a small glimpse of while the shuttle continues to move steadily back and forth.

All the threads for my canvas—also the dark threads of suffering—were perfectly chosen and woven into the fabric of my life, just like they were for Joseph, just like they are for all of God's children. I know that one day, when the weaving of my canvas is complete, and the loom falls silent, that the pattern of my life will be revealed in all its glory. Then I will fully appreciate the role the dark threads played and how they were as needful as the threads of gold and silver. Then I will know in full and *fully* give the Master Weaver the glory He is so deserving of.

In the meantime, I witnessed how other canvases were simultaneously being worked on at the same time as mine. I recognized that some of the dark threads on my loom were noticeable on theirs as well. I belonged to a covenant community and did not live my life in isolation. This is how God ordained things to be. We are the body of Christ of which He is the head (Colossians 1:18) and my journey wasn't a private, individual one.

My dark threads featured in the patterns of other canvases, including those of my husband, my children, my family, my friends, my church community, and many others. This paved the way for many discussions with others, allowing many opportunities to talk about the Master Weaver and the pattern He had for the redemption and restoration of the world.

In this way, God's Word was going out and would not return empty (Isaiah 55:11). There were life-changing conversations. Opportunities arose to give God glory like never before. And isn't that the goal? To live a life where God receives maximum glory? A life where God increases, and we decrease? Countless times, I stood in incredulous amazement at what God accomplished through the opportunities my dark threads afforded. My Weaver imparted a boldness that allowed me to speak of the gold and silver of the gospel to the sick and dying, to the doctors and nurses, and to so many others, a boldness I didn't even know I possessed.

Although I knew that it was God's decision to allow the dark threads in my pattern to simultaneously be woven into the canvases of those around me, I still felt pain at their appearance. Knowing something is needful doesn't mean that it's easy. But I had learned to trust that the Master Weaver had everything planned, everything worked out, for their pattern as well as for mine. It was remarkable to watch Him at work in so many different and varied ways. Not one thread chosen and woven was random or circumstantial.

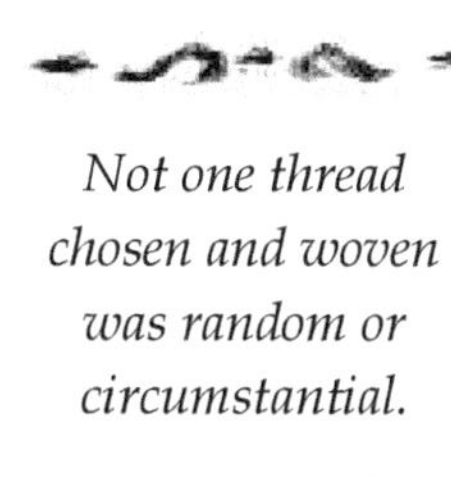
Not one thread chosen and woven was random or circumstantial.

The same was true in the pattern being woven for my children. I saw firsthand how teaching them to trust the Master Weaver with these threads involved actions, not just words. They were watching me very closely, not just listening to what I said about having cancer, but watching how I dealt with it in my day-to-day. I think, perhaps subconsciously, the children were checking to see if my doctrine played out in my life. If what I said, was what I lived. My trust in the Master Weaver impacted their trust. This brought with it a great responsibility. I prayed for enabling grace to display my trust in the Master Weaver to the young canvases being woven around me.

A diary entry I made during my radiation treatment shows my dawning awareness of God intersecting my life with that of so many others:

> I'm starting to see my life as a painting, God working on me in different areas at a time to create a masterpiece ready for the New Jerusalem. But the different recesses of the painting brush others' lives too, and blend in as part of my painting, shaping and forming me, but also so many others. I feel so humbled to be used by God and so humbled that God's light shines in my life and pray His light pierces others' darkness.

> In some ways, the healing of my cancer now seems so secondary compared to the purifying and refining God is doing in my life and the lives around me, also in my immediate family. How can I ever measure the richness of my six-year-old pulling me out of the surf after being dumped by a wave and hearing him say: "That's enough now Mom, come out of the water" or riding his bike beside me when I run, saying: "I know those tears running down your face are from the chemo Mommy." There are brushstrokes everywhere. There is beauty everywhere. There are blessings falling like raindrops. God is touching many others with His brush while painting the story of my life.

How often don't we say we're richly blessed when things go smoothly, when we have a lack of hardships in our lives, when our threads are all gold and silver? Perhaps we have it wrong. Maybe the blessings come through the dark threads interwoven with the gold and silver ones. Maybe the grace comes through understanding that the Master Weaver chooses the perfect threads at the perfect time to complete our canvases in the most perfect way. Perhaps we need to be humbler in accepting His selections and more open to seeing the beauty unmasked by them.

My tears run free when I recall God's weaving of the dark threads of cancer in my life, threads which I would have done anything to stop from appearing at the time. But the more I came to understand the weight and beauty of change accomplished while being woven with them, the more my canvas was formed into a garment of praise (Isaiah 61:3). Praise burst out of me in my conversations with others, praise that seemed unstoppable. I wanted the whole world to know what a wise and loving Weaver God is. I wanted the whole world to see how His sovereignty in the weaving of His patterns showcased His glory, I wanted the whole world to praise Him for His creative beauty. Perhaps, that's my main motivation for writing this book.

But I had many "Jonah moments" along the way, moments where I didn't want to share the beauty of what had been uncovered for me. Moments where going back and reliving the pain was just too difficult. There were also moments where Satan attacked, trying to stop this book from getting in your hands, trying to stop the unstoppable—as he's always done. And the Enemy has power. He tried to interrupt the loom's steady cadence. But he didn't have power to still the loom. He thought he was gaining ground when he saw the dark threads. He was wrong. Nothing and no one can stop the Master Weaver from completing the canvas of His design.

I was safe and secure on my Master Weaver's loom. I was God's handiwork (Ephesians 2:10) and nothing could separate me from His love while He finished what He had begun. "For I am convinced that neither death nor life, neither angels nor demons, neither the present nor the future, nor any powers, neither height nor depth, nor anything else in all creation, will be able to separate us from the love of God that is in Christ Jesus our Lord" (Romans 8:38–39). God was going to complete the canvas He started, complete it for His glory and my good. His Son's own canvas ensured that outcome was achievable.

Really, this is so much more than just about my canvas and my life. It's so much more than about the canvases of those around me. It's so much more than about your canvas, too. Ultimately, this is about a Masterpiece, a Masterpiece being woven by the Master Weaver, connecting all our canvases into the whole—into the greatest canvas of all time. It's the Masterpiece that He has been working on ever since His beautiful canvas of paradise was marred. The canvas of Paradise Restored is being prepared with the final dramatic touches being applied with glory and power (Revelation 15:8), a canvas which will be finished and unrolled soon, when the firmament is rolled back like a scroll.

And on the day of uncovering? All will give the Master Weaver His deserved glory: "'As surely as I live,' says the Lord, 'every knee will bow before me; every tongue will acknowledge God'" (Romans 14:11). God uses the threads He wills, when He wills, and how He wills to accomplish the patterns of our individual canvases and to accomplish the pattern on the great canvas of history.

May the weaving of threads through my life surface in yours through the pages of this book. While the dark threads are being interspersed amongst the silver and gold, may you, too, make the Sovereign LORD your refuge. May you, too, be guided by His counsel, knowing that He holds you by your right hand. May you, too, experience God to be the strength of your heart and your portion forever, even if your flesh and heart may fail.

It is good to be near the Sovereign Weaver, to make Him your refuge. My prayer for you is that, through it all, you, too, in your own way, will tell of all His deeds.

The Master Weaver

My life is but a weaving
Between my Lord and me;
I cannot choose the colors
He worketh steadily.

Oftimes He weaveth sorrow,
And I in foolish pride,
Forget He sees the upper
And I, the underside.

Not till the loom is silent
And the shuttles cease to fly
Shall God unroll the canvas
And explain the reason why

The dark threads are as needful
In the Weaver's skillful hand,
As the threads of gold and silver
In the pattern He has planned.

Author Unknown

Seventeen

The Arrival

And the God of all grace, who called you to His eternal glory in Christ,
after you have suffered a little while,
will Himself restore you and make you strong, firm and steadfast.

1 PETER 5:10

Here we are. Things have finally come full circle. We've arrived.

Well, almost, that is. Maybe we're not quite there yet. But our destination is emerging from the shadows with ever-increasing beauty and glory as we draw continuously closer.

The circle is closing. Not because I'm looking back to the way my life had once been, but rather because I'm looking ahead. Not because I'm going back to who I had once been, but because I'm moving toward all I can be in Christ. Not because I'm walking back to Eden, but because I'm travelling onward to the New Jerusalem. God is bringing me forward in His plan for restoration.

It had been an illusion that closure and restoration was possible this side of eternity. There was to be no paradise here. Sin had marred the perfection of God's creatures and creation and had to be restored. There was no other way but forward.

And, so, God didn't let me go back to who I was, but guided me forward, instead. Forward in my understanding of Who He is and who I am. Forward in my grasp of His glory. Forward in my knowledge of His mercy. Forward in my experience of intimacy with Him. Forward in my restoration as an image bearer of Jesus Christ. Forward on the road to eternal glory. Forward toward a renewal already glimpsed in its infancy through the very cracks of brokenness.

God is continually working toward this great day. Our lives here are but a foretaste, a preparation, for what lays ahead. We are walking the journey God has marked out for each one of us. It's not always the easiest way. But it's the Divine Way, the Only Way, the Way that leads to full restoration and final closure. God always accomplishes His purposes: for me, for you, for the world—in His perfect time, in His perfect way.

True, the tension between the brokenness of this present world and the beauty that awaits in the eternal is still present, but the treasure of discovering the glory of God's restoration plan through His Son Jesus Christ beckons with increased intensity as the plains of disease and suffering are traversed.

This contrast sharpens our vision and gives hope as we discover the beauty that already exists as we travel—a foretaste of the ultimate beauty we will behold upon our arrival. This clearer vision makes the hard sections of the journey worth enduring.

It's a vision that focusses on the depth of sacrifice and suffering made by Jesus Christ on the cross. It's a vision that sees how the ascension of Jesus Christ turned the brokenness of the fall into sin into the beauty of renewal. It's a vision that transforms us into the image in which we were once created. It's a vision that will realize its ultimate fulfillment when Jesus Christ returns on the clouds of heaven, ushering in the completion of the circle,

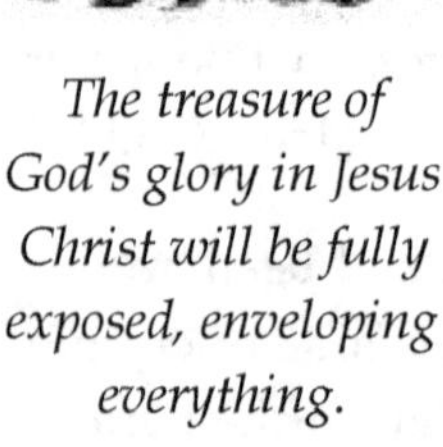

The treasure of God's glory in Jesus Christ will be fully exposed, enveloping everything.

once and for all eternity. Then, with every knee bowing and every tongue confessing (Romans 14:11 NKJV), the treasure of God's glory in Jesus Christ will be fully exposed, enveloping everything.

My vision of God's glory is different now that I'm seeing more clearly than I did before. Then I remembered. The "glory" card! The one I received from a friend shortly after my breast cancer diagnosis. The card that simply read:

May God receive the glory.

It was a card with a message I didn't get—at first. Now, I got it. Now I understood that life is all about God's glory in my story and my delight in Him through that story. Now I understood that through His glory, my joy is made complete.

God is the Author, the Completer, the Finisher, the Perfector. The Beginning and the End. The Glorious One. We are the fallen. The rescued. The redeemed. The restored. The righteous. Realizing our fallen state and seeing the glorious restoration God is accomplishing fills us with great rejoicing!

Now I can appreciate fully the words of Jonathan Edwards, written so long ago: "God is glorified not only by His glory's being seen, but by its being rejoiced in. When those that see it delight in it, God is more glorified than if they only see it. His glory is then received by the whole soul, both by the understanding and by the heart."[61]

When our hearts truly delight in God's glory, we can only respond with humiliation of self and glorification of God. Charles Spurgeon described it perfectly:

> It is clear, then, that self must stand out of the way, that there may be room for God to be exalted; and this is the reason, the true secret, why God bringeth his people ofttimes into straits and difficulties, that, being brought to their wits' end, and made conscious of their own folly and weakness, they may be

---

61 Edwards, *Works of Jonathan Edwards, Volume 13*, 495.

> fitted to behold the majesty of God when He comes forth to work their deliverance.
>
> Your troubles have enriched you with a wealth of knowledge to be gained by no other means: your trials have been the cleft of the rock in which God has set you, as He did his servant Moses, that you might behold His glory as it passed by. Praise your God, O sons of sorrow, ye have not been left to the darkness and ignorance which continued prosperity might have involved. Bless Him that you have been capacitated to show forth His glory by being permitted and honoured to endure a great fight of affliction.[62]

I had been capacitated, made ready, for the outshinings of His glory! This foretaste I received had led to an excitement and anticipation of what was still to come when the circle of restoration would be ushered in. Seeing dimly, knowing in part, was already so glorious. I could hardly imagine what it would be like to see clearly and to know fully. "For now we see only a reflection as in a mirror; then we shall see face to face. Now I know in part; then I shall know fully, even as I am fully known" (1 Corinthians 13:12).

And so, we see the circle closing up ahead. Our dawn of eternity will begin when the time has fully come, the time when "He comes to be glorified in His holy people and to be marveled at among all those who have believed" (2 Thessalonians 1:10). On that day we will see Jesus Christ in all His Kingly Glory, and then we will know the complete story.

Why can't this day come sooner? Because restoration is a process, a process that involves a journey from here to There. A journey that takes time, gives us time—time to travel, time to change, time to anticipate. That's why we don't arrive overnight. J.C. Ryle once wrote: "There was a direct road from Egypt to Canaan, yet Israel was not led into it; but round through the wilderness. And this seemed hard at the time."[63] We may not understand our difficult route. But God is perfect and His route and His timing are perfect,

---

[62] Spurgeon, "Direction in Dilemma," Metropolitan Tabernacle Pulpit, Volume 9.
[63] Ryle, *The Duties of Parents*, 26.

leading to the perfect destination at the perfect time. We just need to follow Him.

It's so much bigger than my or your individual story, isn't it? It always has been. When we widen our gaze, we see it: His story in our story and His glory in that story. Suffering helps us to grasp it, causes us to pause and truly experience the wonder of it all. Our suffering encourages us to become glory-seekers—not our glory, but God's! And then, amazingly, as we seek His glory, we become partakers of this very same glory by His Spirit dwelling within our broken vessels. We shine that glory more and more as we behold Him more and more. The family resemblance increases simultaneously with our transformation. It's what 1 John 3:2 promises: "Dear friends, now we are children of God, and what we will be has not yet been made known. But we know that when Christ appears, we shall be like Him, for we shall see Him as He is."

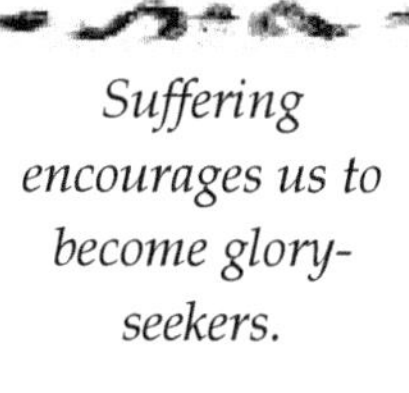

Your story doesn't end here. In fact, your story doesn't end. So, travel onward, dear heart. The gates of the LORD through which the righteous can enter are just up ahead (Psalm 118:20). You know: the ones made of pearl, beautifully luminous in their completeness, reminding all who enter that their re-creation is finished.

> 'Come, I will show you the bride, the wife of the Lamb.' And he carried me away in the Spirit to a mountain great and high, and showed me the Holy City, Jerusalem, coming down out of heaven from God. It shone with the glory of God, and its brilliance was like that of a very precious jewel, like a jasper, clear as crystal. It had a great, high wall with twelve gates, and with twelve angels at the gates. On the gates were written the names of the twelve tribes of Israel. The twelve gates were twelve pearls, each gate made of a single pearl. The great street of the city was of gold, as pure as transparent glass. The glory and honor of the nations will be brought into it (Revelation 21:9–12, 21, 26).

All that will be left for me and for you is to enter in. So, when the time has fully come, I will see you there, my brothers, my sisters. Let's gather at the gates made of pearl and glorify the King of Glory together, forever, in unending joyful perfection, joining all the saints who have gone before. Paradise will have been restored.

Everything will have come full circle. There will be no more broken.

Only beauty. For all eternity.

The Circle

Back in the summer days, 2014 the year
My life's story was halted; my mind paralyzed by fear.
Cancer was diagnosed, tears were shed
As God took my hand and me His child led.

Through rivers and fire and valleys we went
While teaching me time and again on Him to depend.
Refuge was sought in the shelter of His wings
As I more and more to Him began to cling.

His ever present help was always near –
As time marched along He allayed my fears.
The mountains plunged, the earth did shake
But my Rock stood firm as higher places we did take.

Angels were given charge over me
Ensuring the terrors of night would flee.
Many prayers were offered to the throne room of God;
His mercy so often tearfully sought.

Doctors' hands were prayed over; nurses showed love
As never before help was sought from above.
Four months later the worst days seemed done –
The cancer, it appeared, its course had run.

It was then that I realized I was grieving my loss
As I came to terms with my body's paying the cost.
"God," I asked, "is this the new me?
Is this the woman you want me to be?

Why do I feel such a shadow of self?
Your creation of me has been marred," I deeply felt.
So back to the corridors of the medical world I went;
My days in the theatre had not yet been spent.

November 2015, with the summer just dawning
Saw my heart full of hope, coming full circle its longing.
Surgeons' hands once again were blessed by my Father –
This time not to remove, but to restore His daughter.

Making it through, closure appeared in sight;
I was more than ready to leave behind cancer's blight.
But my plans weren't God's; my will not His;
It seemed I had more to learn as in His presence I lived.

Cancer once again its terrible head did rear
The words radiating shockwaves, but this time no fear.
I knew that God stood beside me that day;
With the circle reopened I was about to re-enter the fray.

I was thankful this cancer was found so amazingly;
Who would have known otherwise where time would've taken me?
So through the shock, confusion, and pain
I also saw God's Hand, with sunshine through the rain.

Once again it was hard telling family and friends
That no one was sure where this journey would end.
Up close and personal, God's sovereignty was felt;
At times it seemed that too hard a hand had been dealt.

But as all things believed were put to the test
God's provisions were there, and my heart found its rest.
I knew this was not the end of my journey as yet
And that more raindrops of blessing had to be spent.

So back to the trenches I returned;
Hand in hand through the desert God and I sojourned.
Complete and total reliance on Him
Would prove the only way to come through and win.

Endless days of treatments were endured
As I was spiritually being matured –
learning to see that life from God was a gift;
Something to be cherished, and not something merely lived.

Hard times came when my two cousins died;
Their bodies succumbed to cancer, but their spirits arrived
In heaven above as they received their crowns
And were adorned with their beautiful white gowns.

As I continued to press onward with God molding my soul
I began to reach an understanding of suffering's goal:
The refining God was doing in my life
Was to make me more beautiful in His sight!

Through many a day I was carried on Eagle's wings
And glimpsed the glory that one day He would bring.
I stood amazed at the Light I beheld;
While seeking God's face, nothing seemed withheld.

Late in May 2016 the day finally dawned
When treatments were done and no cancer was found.
But closure no longer held the lure it once offered;
In its place something much more beautiful was proffered.

A heart full of thankfulness for what God had done:
Granting me the gift of His Spirit and Son –
Showing His love to me in intimate ways;
Teaching me what's important is not length of days.

But rather the goal is to seek God's face
And dwell in His light and live by His grace.
So as I begin the next chapter of my story
My soul rejoices and gives Him all the glory.

The ending of my book will one day come
Where I will live happily ever after, my journey: done.
In the meantime I travel onward, ever looking above
And enjoy each day in the light of God's love.

Helena Bolhuis

November 7, 2015
edited June 24, 2016

With thanks . . .

It's hard to have a "thanks" page, because there are so many to thank! So, to all of you who have been there for me, supporting me with love and prayer through my cancer journey and the writing of this book, I give God thanks for you.

To my husband: I will always love you! The journey was ours to take together as we were refined, and I thank God for your presence in my life and heart. Twenty-five years ago, you pledged to be true to me in sickness and in health and you kept your vow and have done so much more besides. You are a man of integrity. Thank you—for everything.

To my children: You are all my sunshine and you'll never know how much I love you . . . now and forever. Continue to shine like stars as you go your way to the end.

To my Mom & Dad and Mum & Dad: Who could ask for more? Being raised to fear the LORD is an irreplaceable provision of God's grace. Thanks for walking alongside, encouraging, praying for, and loving our family.

To my brothers and sisters and extended family, most of whom were unrelenting with their love and prayers: Thank you.

To my various pastors and their wives, for always reminding me of all my treasures in Christ: Your treasures are stored up for you in heaven. Thank you for always being there.

To Rev K, who guided me spiritually through my desert march: Your messages of hope from God's Word flavor this book and my life. You were a willing provision from my Father, and I sincerely thank you.

To my church family and friends: You were amazing, from baking, cooking, cleaning, weeding, driving, sending flowers and cards, but most of all by praying. You went all out in showing me the love of Christ. A special thanks to my Perth and Albany friends who made the trek to Burekup time and again. And to those few for whom being there was just too hard—may it be different for you the next time around.

To my doctors and nurses who were the hands and feet of the Great Physician: My heartfelt thanks for your compassionate care.

To the kind staff at Solaris Cancer Care: Thank you for gifting me the mind space to meditate and renew along cancer's hard road.

To a dear Oom & Tante who prayed me through the days and months of writing and editing this book: Without your prayers I'm not sure when or if I would have even begun, much less crossed the finish line!

To my three country friends whose threads were woven closely with mine: I thank God for your courage to just show up, not to mention the myriad of things you did in addition to that. You truly put Job's three friends to shame!

To my newfound city friends: Thanking God for His provision in this new chapter of my life.

To my publisher: Thank you for letting these words see the light of day.

To my two editors: Thank you for coming into the antechambers and for doing such great work there. You make a formidable team.

To my cover designer: How can I ever forget the morning where the idea for the amazing book cover was born?

To my two dear cousins Caroline and Nellie who are clothed in their white garments and have received their crowns: I miss you! Till we meet again.

To my Father: Thank You for carrying me on Eagle's wings. The view as we soared was glorious. See You soon.

Bibliography

Anglo-Genevan Psalter (Revised Edition). Winnipeg, Manitoba: Premier Printing, 1984.

Augustine of Hippo. *"The Confessions of St. Augustine (1766)."* Orleans, Massachusetts: Paraclete Press, 2010.

Bunyan, John. *The Works of John Bunyan, Volume 2,* (edited by George Offor). Edinburgh: Banner of Truth, 1991.

Edwards, Jonathan. *The Works of Jonathan Edwards, Volume 13,* (edited by Thomas A. Schafer). New Haven, Connecticut: Yale University Press, 1994.

Elliot, Elisabeth. *Suffering is Never for Nothing*. Nashville: Broadman & Holman, 2019.

Gould, Leslie, and Mindy Starns Clarke. *The Amish Nanny*. Eugene, Oregon: Harvest House, 2011.

Hawks, Annie. "I Need Thee Ev'ry Hour." 1872.

Keats, John. "Letters of John Keats." London: Macmillan, 1891.

Lee, Jennifer. *A Moment to Breathe*. Tennessee: Lifeway Christian Resources, 2017.

Lewis, C.S. *The Last Battle*. New York: Macmillan, 1956.
———*Letters of C.S. Lewis*. New York: Harcourt Brace Jovanovich, 1975.
———*Mere Christianity – Fiftieth Anniversary Edition*. London: HarperCollins, 2002.
———*The Problem of Pain*. London: Collins, 2012.

———*The Screwtape Letters*. London: HarperCollins Religious, 1998.
———*The Weight of Glory*. New York: Macmillan, 1949.

Merriam-Webster Online. http://www.merriam-webster.com/.

Moore, Thomas. *The Comforter*. http://artandtheology.org/tag/thomas-moore/.

Owen, John. *The Glory of Christ*. Edinburgh: Banner of Truth, 1994.

Piper, John. *Don't Waste Your Life*. Wheaton, Illinois: Crossway, 2009.
——— "What Is God's Glory?" http://www.desiringgod.org/interviews/what-is-gods-glory--2.

Piper, John, et al. *Suffering and the Sovereignty of God*. Wheaton, Illinois: Crossway, 2006.

Ryle, J.C. *The Duties of Parents*. Sand Springs, Oklahoma: Grace & Truth Books, 2002.
———*Expository Thoughts on Luke: Volume 2*. Edinburgh: Banner of Truth, 1986.

Silk, Susan and Barry Goldman. "The Ring Theory." http://www.psychologytoday.com/au/blog/promoting-hope-preventing-suicide/201705/ring-theory-helps-us-bring-comfort-in.

Spurgeon, C. "Direction in Dilemma." http://www.spurgeon.org/resource-library/sermons/direction-in-dilemma#flipbook/.
——— "He shall be Great." http://www.spurgeon.org/resource-library/sermons/he-shall-be-great#flipbook/.

——— "The Secret of Power in Prayer."
http://www.spurgeon.org/resource-library/sermons/the-secret-of-power-in-prayer#flipbook/.
——— "Terrible Convictions and Gentle Drawings."
http://www.ccel.org/ccel/spurgeon/sermons06/sermons06.xxvii.html.
——— "Why the Heavenly Robes are White."
http://www.ccel.org/ccel/spurgeon/sermons22.xlvi.html.
——— "Woe and Weal."
http://www.spurgeongems.org/sermon/chs3239.pdf.

Story, Laura, "Blessings." Track 5 on *Blessings*. INO Records, 2011, compact disc.

Strong's Exhaustive Concordance Online. http://biblehub.com/hebrew/2803.htm.

Teellinck, Willem. *The Path of True Godliness*. Grand Rapids: Reformation Heritage Books, 2006.

ten Boom, Corrie. "Corrie ten Boom Quotes." http://www.goodreads.com/author/quotes/102203.Corrie_ten_Boom.

Tippetts, Kara. *The Hardest Peace*. Colorado Springs: David C. Cook, 2014.
——— "Sacrifice of Thanksgiving".
http://www.mundanefaithfulness.com/home/2015/1/6/sacrifice-of-thanksgiving.

Tippetts, Kara, and Jill Lynn Buteyn (Contributor) *Just Show Up*. Colorado Springs: David C. Cook, 2015.

Voskamp, Ann. *The Broken Way*. Grand Rapids: Zondervan, 2016.

——— "Dear Little Lies that are keeping us up late." http://m.facebook.com/AnnVoskamp/photos/a.369461463066034.92483.324577877554393/1144809072197932/?type=3&__tn__=C-R.

———*The Way of Abundance: A 60-Day Journey into a Deeply Meaningful Life.* Grand Rapids: Zondervan, 2018.

Westerink, H. *Call Upon Me.* Fergus, Ontario: Inter-League, 1986.

Westminster Assembly. *Westminster Shorter Catechism*, 1646–1647.

Wolfe, Paul D. *My God is True!* Edinburgh: Banner of Truth, 2009.